OCCULTISTS AND MYSTICS
OF ALL AGES

OCCULTISTS & MYSTICS OF ALL AGES

BY
RALPH SHIRLEY

New Foreword by
LESLIE SHEPARD

WITH FOUR ILLUSTRATIONS

THE CITADEL PRESS   SECAUCUS, NEW JERSEY

First paperbound printing, 1974
Copyright © 1972 by University Books Inc.
All rights reserved
— Published by Citadel Press
A division of Lyle Stuart, Inc.
120 Enterprise Ave., Secaucus, N.J. 07094
In Canada: George J. McLeod Limited
73 Bathurst St., Toronto 2B, Ontario
Manufactured in the United States of America
ISBN 0-8065-0419-6

CONTENTS

CHAP.		PAGE
1. APOLLONIUS OF TYANA	. . . . .	2
2. PLOTINUS	. . . . . .	31
3. MICHAEL SCOTT	. . . . .	54
4. PARACELSUS	. . . . . .	76
5. EMANUEL SWEDENBORG	. . . .	91
6. COUNT CAGLIOSTRO	. . . .	120
7. ANNA KINGSFORD	. . . . .	145

ILLUSTRATIONS

	FACING PAGE
PARACELSUS	78
EMANUEL SWEDENBORG	92
COUNT CAGLIOSTRO	122
ANNA KINGSFORD	146

NEW FOREWORD

In every age, people have been inspired by the great mystics and occult personalities of their time.

Mystics and occultists bridge that mysterious gap between man and the enigmatic divine infinity from which he comes. Such rare individuals are channels for knowledge inaccessible to ordinary men and women; they also unlock powers and secrets of nature denied to most of us.

The present book discusses seven of these great personalities of former times, from the first century A.D. to the end of the nineteenth century. Here are stories of great men and women who sought secret knowledge and mystical insights.

Apollonius, once regarded as a serious rival to Jesus Christ and worshiped as a god, is little known nowadays. In appearance he was not unlike a modern hippy, being long-haired and barefooted. He was also a strict vegetarian. But he possessed a dignity and power that arose from an inner sense of truth, wisdom, and beauty rather than from his appearance. He traveled throughout the known world of his time and worked many miracles. A believer in reincarnation, he claimed that he had been a humble ship's pilot in a previous existence. He made a tremendous impression on the world in which he lived, but vanished without a definite testament beyond the marvelous legends that have come down to us. This compact assessment of a great figure of the early Christian era usefully complements the full-length study *Apollonius of Tyana* by G. R. S. Mead (University Books Inc., 1966).

ii   OCCULTISTS & MYSTICS OF ALL AGES

Plotinus, a mystic of the following century, gave the world a profound philosophy of origins, and his lectures are still quoted today for their great metaphysical insight. Like Apollonius he was also credited with miraculous powers. Such was his influence that the Emperor Gallineus proposed to establish an ideal community based on his philosophy, to be called "Platonopolis." Unfortunately the scheme fell through following the death of Plotinus. The teachings of Plotinus have exerted a powerful influence long after his passing, for he was not merely a theorist. His descriptions of the transcendental bliss of the mystic in absorption with the divine source of God are drawn from personal experience. His disciple Porphyry recorded that Plotinus attained this ecstatic union several times during the six years he studied with him.

Michael Scot, romanticized as a wizard in Sir Walter Scott's fanciful poem "Lay of the Last Minstrel," was more occultist than mystic. He was a noted mathematician, alchemist, and astrologer, around whom wonderful legends of magical power circulated. Scot distinguished himself by translating important philosophical and mathematical works from the Arabic, thus extending European scholarship. One of his books contains a specific formula for making gold. Scot was also a noted physician and treated the poor free of charge. He is said to have foretold the manner of his own death.

Paracelsus was one of the greatest doctors and surgeons of his time, and his experiments with "magnetic healing" anticipated Mesmer and hypnotism. He was born about the time that Columbus discovered America, and his colorful life uncovered a new world of medical treatment. Samuel Hahnemann, the founder of modern homeopathy, based his system on the theories and experiments of Paracelsus. Chemist, mining expert, natural scientist, and physician, Paracelsus lived during the Reformation of Luther and the renaissance of classical ideals and scholarship. It was a period when the powerful influence of the invention of printing was beginning to affect the whole current of European studies. The marvelous cures of Paracelsus earned him a reputation as an occultist in some quarters and mountebank in others. He insisted on the importance of spiritual life as a factor in health. His radical theories and impressive achievements galvanized the thought of his time.

Swedenborg was undoubtedly a most versatile genius. Experienced in lens grinding, map engraving, military fortification, organ playing, factory organization, chemistry, sociology, and many other specialized branches of knowledge, he could have been the leading scientist of his day. He even speculated on the invention of submarines and flying machines. But he went on to crown a brilliant practical life by the development of mediumistic faculties, and developed a mystical system which survives at the present day.

Cagliostro is perhaps the most colorful figure of eighteenth-century intrigue, and still remains a profound mystery. Occultist, Freemason, wonder-worker, diplomat, he was a generous, noble, and mysterious personage. He was finally a victim of the venomous spite of the arch-villain De Moreau, center of the great intrigues of the day. Was Cagliostro really the adventurer called Joseph Balsamo, or was this a cruel slander to destroy his reputation? Whatever the facts of his mysterious origins, he became a legend in his lifetime.

Anna Kingsford, a modern mystic, developed her own kind of Mystical Christianity together with her husband Edward Maitland. An early champion of women's rights, she passionately believed that justice between men and women would be possible only by women "magnifying their womanhood and not by exchanging it for a factitious masculinity." She also campaigned against cruelty to animals in the name of science. Her lone cult of mysticism was somewhat overshadowed by the more romantically colorful activities of Madame Blavatsky and the Theosophical Society, but her doctrine of women's rights has special relevance today.

These, then, are a handful of remarkable individuals singled out by writer Ralph Shirley.

Ralph Shirley (1865-1946), who describes the life and thought of these remarkable people, was also an unusual person. Hardly a mystic, he was a gentleman scholar fascinated by mysticism and the occult, with special training in astrology. As editor of the celebrated journal *The Occult Review,* which he founded in 1905, he gathered around him the leading occultists, mystics, and magicians of his day. The journal appeared under Shirley's editorship for twenty years. The names of the contributors have since become legendary. Arthur Edward Waite, Dr. Franz Hartmann, Andrew Lang, Aleister Crowley, Miss A. Goodrich-Freer, Hereward Carrington, W. J. Brodie-Innes, Lady Archibald Campbell, H. Stanley Redgrove, "Oliver Fox," Lewis Spence, and many other talented personalities contributed important articles on every aspect of occultism, while Shirley himself wrote a wise and tolerant editorial every month. Shirley first publicized reports of Astral Projection, then a relatively unknown field of occultism, and his book *The Mystery of the Human Double* (reissued by University Books Inc.) is still one of the best introductions to the subject. (In my Foreword to this reissue I have given a more detailed sketch of Shirley himself.)

It was most unfortunate that Shirley was obliged to resign editorship of the journal which he had created when it changed hands in 1925. The new proprietors did not even print his farewell address (although already set in type) and many readers must have been puzzled by his departure. Shirley had written that he hoped he could claim that his journal "has at least partially achieved its aim of raising the standard of Occult and Psychic investigation to a higher level and of drawing together the more intellectual spirits interested in the subjects with which it has dealt, by affording a common platform on which they could write for the furtherance of a movement which is yet destined to play a leading part in evolving to a higher and more spiritual level the humanity of our Twentieth Century world."

The present book was first published in 1920, and like all Shirley's writing it is clear, thoughtful, scholarly, and reads as well today as fifty years ago.

Although the book comprises seven self-contained studies, they are connected by the philosophical background of Shirley's own viewpoint. Most of the characters of whom he writes had in common the powerful influence of Neoplatonism, that metaphysical impulse that reinterpreted ancient religion and bridged Eastern and Western philosophy in its quest for awareness beyond the material world. The impulse of occultism is something of a counterpart that at best provided a sound material basis for mysticism, at worst led to superstition and perverse cultism. In modern times little of the mystical impulse has survived in a world devoted almost exclusively to the material side of things. Since this book was first published, there have been many self-styled mystics with a spurious chemical ecstasy, but there is no true inspiration in self-deception and addiction.

One must learn to distinguish between the true and false in mysticism, among the mass-media mail-order *gurus* who try to make a pop religion out of what should be a humble and unsensational way of life. For the urge for fame and ego gratification takes many forms, and there is real estate in metaphysics. I have listened to enthusiastic reports of great world movements with thousands of paying members, have been proudly shown charts and graphs of national branches and group leaders. Such *gurus* are only the Bernie Cornfelds of metaphysics. Compared with the clear insight and high intellectual standards of Shirley's time, present-day pop cults are vulgar and confused, riddled with egoism and self-deception.

Yet the true mystical impulse is basic to the human situation, and always reappears just when one thinks it has been lost forever. Only the validation of the mystical experience itself can provide a groundwork for everyday life and conduct, since the rise and fall of the property game leads to wars and spiritual degeneration. The old-fashioned code of elementary morals was the first stage of purification in developing higher consciousness. Power, money, fame, ego, and hedonism are the oldest temptations in the world, and they are very seductive, but they lead to ever-increasing world holocausts. Man learns only slowly by trial and error that no gain in the material world can match even the smallest awareness of mystical consciousness.

The present book tells the story of marvelous people and timeless teachings. It forms an excellent companion volume to *Modern Mystics* by Sir Francis Younghusband (University Books Inc., 1970).

And for those who still find it difficult to believe that there is a place in modern life for mysticism, I would quote the words of Pandit Gopi Krishna, a modern mystic who attained higher consciousness, and who has now attracted the interest of enlightened scientists:

NEW FOREWORD

The human mind is so constituted that no luxury and no treasure of the earth can assuage its burning fever seeking an explanation for its own existence. All the heavy weight of this inscrutable mystery, all the questions posed by intellect, all the suffering of the harrowing ascent of evolution, all the pain felt at the injustice and misery prevailing in the world, all the disappointment of shattered dreams and broken hopes, all the anguish of eternal partings from near and dear ones, and all the fear of ill health, decay and death—vanish like vapor at the rise of the inner Sun, at the recognition of the inmost Self, beyond thought, beyond doubt, beyond pain, beyond mortality which, once perceived, illumines the darkness of the mind as a flash of strong lightning cleaves the darkness of the night, leaving man transformed with but one glimpse of the inexpressible splendor and glory of the spiritual world. May this sublime knowledge become accessible to all. May there come enlightenment and peace to the minds of all. *

1971   LESLIE SHEPARD

*Quoted by kind permission of Kundalini Research Foundation, 440 East 62nd Street, New York, N. Y. 10021.

OCCULTISTS AND MYSTICS
OF ALL AGES

OCCULTISTS & MYSTICS OF ALL AGES

I

APOLLONIUS OF TYANA

THE difficulty of treating of such a subject as the life and activities of the Philosopher of Tyana lies in the fact that the story of Apollonius's career has been overlaid with legends of the miraculous on the one hand, and distorted by religious prejudices on the other; while the only authoritative account of this great religious reformer is marred by the glaring deficiencies of the writer for the task which he had in hand, and his inability to appreciate the life-work of the subject of his biography. Indeed he fills many pages with literary padding of the worst kind, while he fails to give us over and over again the very facts which it is of value and importance for us to know. Philostratus, the author of this life, was one of the literary coterie that gathered round the presiding genius of the Empress Julia Domna, the wife of Septimus Severus and mother of Caracalla. Julia Domna was a generous patroness of art and literature, and her husband Severus was devoted to the study of occult science. Gibbon, in his usual sceptical vein, observes that " he was passionately addicted to the vain studies of magic and divination, deeply versed in the interpretation of dreams and omens, and perfectly acquainted with the science of judicial astrology." The Empress, who was a daughter of the Priest of the Sun at Emesa in Syria, was an enthusiastic bibliophile and had collected, among her other literary treasures, the note-books of Damis, the companion and fellow traveller of Apollonius. These note-books or tablets contained the records of his journeys and other details concerning the life of Apollonius, who was as great a hero to Damis as ever Johnson was to Boswell. If these notes were as full of detail as Philostratus asserts, one can only regret that the biographer did not turn them to more useful account. Damis was a native of Ninus or Nineveh, and Philostratus speaks somewhat contemptuously of his defective Greek style. But it is probable that with all their grammatical errors the note-books of Damis would have given us a truer portrait of the great philosopher than the more finished phrases and elaborate oratorical devices of Philostratus. The biographer had also access to a book written by Maximus of Ægæ, containing a record of Apollonius's doings at that place. It requires an acute critic to gauge how much of Philostratus's narrative is literary embellishment and interpolated matter, and how much is actually derived from the original records. Even the Gospels of the Evangelists hardly present a more difficult task to the critic anxious to discriminate between the original and the glosses with which it is overlaid.

The other difficulty from which the record of Apollonius's life and teachings has suffered is due to the religious disputes which arose through the rapid growth of Christianity and its conflict with the previously existing religions of the Roman world. We may argue legitimately enough that the power of working miracles is no proof of the truth of the doctrines expounded by any religious teacher. But the fact remains that in proselytising for Christianity the fullest use was made of the miracles recorded as accomplished by Jesus in the Gospels, in support of the contention in favour of the Divine origin of their worker, and of his work. Illogical though this argument may appear to the philosophic mind, it is not surprising that it should have carried great weight, and indeed it must be admitted that it does so even at the present day. What more natural, then, than that one of the disputants on the other side should have produced a polemical pamphlet in which he attempted to show that such an argument was a two-edged weapon, and that in fact it was possible to produce better evidence in favour of the miracles attributed to the pagan philosopher Apollonius than for those of Jesus of Nazareth, and to argue that, this being the case, even assuming the authenticity of the Gospel narrative, there was no more justification for regarding the Jewish prophet as a God than the Tyanian philosopher? Such a criticism of the claims of the Christians was in fact written by Hierocles, a philosopher of some note and successively governor of Palmyra, Bithynia, and Alexandria, about the first decade of the fourth century A.D., under the title of *Philalethes*, or *The Truth-lover*.

This pamphlet was not long in provoking a rejoinder from a leading light of the Christian community. The reply, the author of which was Eusebius, Bishop of Cæsarea, is still extant, though Hierocles's contribution to the controversy was destroyed, like much other evidence hostile to Christianity, by the ecclesiastical authorities, when the new religion finally became triumphant. Eusebius was able to show that Philostratus was not a reliable authority, and that his judgment, where the credibility of a narrative was in question, was clearly at fault. Though the criticisms of Eusebius might have been applied with equal force to much of the Gospel record, it is plain that his retort to

APOLLONIUS OF TYANA

Hierocles did not lack point, the veracity of Philostratus being obviously not above suspicion, and some of his narratives urgently calling for evidential corroboration, indeed, in certain cases, being mere legend or romance. This applies in especial to the account given of Apollonius's journey to India, which is interspersed with numerous fantastic stories which appear to be derived by Philostratus from other sources and interpolated in an unscrupulous manner, with the idea, presumably, of giving local colour. There are, however, numerous records given which are clearly taken direct from the narrative of Damis, and the general accuracy of which there appears to be no adequate reason to call in question. One of these offers a parallel to the various accounts of the raising of the dead to life given in the Gospel story, as, for instance, the recalling to life of the son of the widow of Nain ; the raising from the dead of Jairus's daughter, and last but not least, the case of Martha and Mary's brother Lazarus, which, owing to the circumstances surrounding it, has caught hold of the popular imagination to a greater extent than either of the others. The record of the incident referred to is given in Philostratus's life [1] as follows :—

Here, too, is a miracle which Apollonius worked : A girl

---
[1] *Philostratus*, Book IV, chapter xlv. I am indebted to Dr Conybeare's translation, published by Messrs Heinemann, for this and some other quotations. The book is a very useful one, the Greek and English being given side by side.

had died just in the hour of her marriage, and the bridegroom was following her bier lamenting, as was natural, his marriage left unfulfilled, and the whole of Rome was mourning with him, for the maiden belonged to a consular family. Apollonius then witnessing their grief, said: " Put down the bier, for I will stay the tears that you are shedding for this maiden." And withal he asked what was her name. The crowd accordingly thought that he was about to deliver such an oration as is commonly delivered as much to grace the funeral as to stir up lamentation; but he did nothing of the kind, but merely touching her and whispering in secret some spell over her, at once woke up the maiden from her seeming death; and the girl spoke out loud, and returned to her father's house, just as Alcestis did when she was brought back to life by Hercules. And the relations of the maiden wanted to present him with the sum of 150,000 sesterces, but he said that he would freely present the money to the young lady by way of dowry. Now, whether he detected some spark of life in her, which those who were nursing her had not noticed —for it is said that although it was raining at the time, a vapour went up from her face—or whether life was really extinct, and he restored it by the warmth of his touch, is a mysterious problem which neither I myself nor those who were present could decide.

The record of this incident is presumably taken direct from the notes of Damis, and is not, I think, to be too lightly set aside. Apollonius does not appear to have made any claim to supernatural power in the matter, nor need he be necessarily credited with anything beyond an intuitive capacity for divining the fact that life had not finally departed. Nor indeed are we bound to assume

APOLLONIUS OF TYANA

anything more than this intuitive capacity as regards the two first-mentioned miracles in the Gospel records—those of the son of the widow of Nain and Jairus's daughter. The raising of Lazarus may be held to stand in a different category, but it is noteworthy as regards this, that only one Evangelist records the incident and that his Gospel is the latest in date of the four. This has naturally not escaped the attention of the critics, as it is almost incredible that neither Matthew, Mark, nor Luke should have alluded to so sensational an incident if they had any knowledge of its occurrence. On the other hand, so dramatic an event could hardly have failed to excite the greatest commotion at the time, and must, one would naturally have supposed, inevitably have reached the ears of those who were writing biographies of the performer of the miracle. The incident, in short, is hardly one that could be placed even on the same evidential plane as the raising of the consul's daughter at Rome by Apollonius.

The problem as to whether life is, or is not, extinct in any specific instance has over and over again proved too difficult of solution for even the ablest of modern doctors, and in cases of trance, opinions of the medical profession can be freely cited that there is no apparent difference to be detected between the living and the dead.

Numerous tests have been applied and failed in cases where the patient has eventually regained consciousness, and it is legitimate to suppose that a certain clairvoyant power is in some cases alone capable of determining the possibility of the spirit returning to reoccupy its mortal tenement. According to occult theory, if the chord or magnetic link that unites the astral with the physical body has not been definitely severed, it is still possible for life to be restored. What more probable than that one gifted with abnormal psychical powers, such as either Jesus or Apollonius, might diagnose the presence of this connecting link, which was invisible to all around ?

Eusebius argues that the stories told of Apollonius's psychic powers detract from his credit as a philosopher. Such powers, he argues, only appertain to a divine being, and therefore while they may be justly credited in the case of Jesus they must be dismissed in that of Apollonius. Such arguments will hardly appeal to the unbiased critic of the present day. We must recognise, however, that it was Philostratus's methods of embellishing his narrative with fantastic oriental and other legends which gave a loophole for the attack of Eusebius. There was, indeed, a sufficiently serious sequel to this early passage of arms. The discussion as to whether or not Apollonius's miracles were entitled to be set in juxaposition to

APOLLONIUS OF TYANA

those of the Prophet of Nazareth, proved in the end to be a veritable red-herring drawn across the track of the whole story of Apollonius's life and labours. Though there is no recorded reference of Apollonius to Jesus or his teachings, he is made to appear in the light of subsequent controversies as the false prophet *par excellence*, and worker of pseudo-miracles, sent by the devil, according to one ingenious commentator, to destroy the work of the Saviour by an attempt to imitate his miracles, and thus to disprove their unique character. When the printing press came into vogue and classical literature was widely disseminated by this means, Aldus hesitated to print the text of Philostratus's *Life of Apollonius*, and only did so finally with the text of Eusebius's treatise added as an appendix, so that, as he phrased it, "the antidote might accompany the poison." Later on, ingenious Continental commentators advanced the theory that the life of Apollonius was a myth, and that it had for its object the defence of classical philosophy as opposed to Christianity. This theory is as ingenious as it is unconvincing, and even the authority of its defenders, Baur and Zeller, has failed to secure it a serious hearing at the present day. It is obvious that the supposed antagonism between Jesus and Apollonius never really existed at all, and though probably they were born within twenty years of each other, there is no evidence to show that there was any connection of any kind between their respective lives and activities.

The tradition which credits Apollonius with being a worker of miracles and magician is widespread, but there is comparatively little that is narrated of him by Philostratus which is incredible, if assumed to have been performed by a man who had led a life such as that of the Sage of Tyana, and who was gifted with such psychic powers as we are familiar with at the present day. We shall probably be right in regarding most of these narratives of psychic incidents as taken direct from the tablets of Damis, and therefore in the main authentic, even if the details are not in every case exact. A few instances will serve to illustrate the point of what I have said.

After Apollonius's visit to Athens, in which he was initiated into the Eleusinian Mysteries, he took ship for Egypt, stopping at Rhodes on the way. Arriving at Alexandria he found that his reputation had preceded him, and was met everywhere with reverence and respect. He took advantage of the friendly popular feeling towards him to intervene in a case of miscarriage of justice. A robbery had recently taken place in the town, and twelve men had been condemned in connection with it. An innocent victim of the general sentence was revealed psychically to Apollonius. He thereupon called the procession to a halt as they were being led to execution, and instructed the guard to place the innocent man last of the twelve. The delay thus secured gave time for a horseman to ride up with a reprieve for the man in question, whose innocence had been established subsequently to the trial. It is not difficult to attribute such a case as this to psychic powers, but, on the other hand, it is quite open to us to assume that Apollonius had learned something by normal means as to the doubt hanging over the condemned man's implication in the crime.

Never, perhaps, has any possessor of noted psychic powers enjoyed the friendship or the hostility of so many great Emperors as did Apollonius. Vespasian and Titus were both intimate in their friendship, and sought the advice of the sage of Tyana on various notable occasions. It was, it appears, during this same visit to Alexandria that Vespasian arrived at the great Egyptian seaport and requested an interview with the sage. Vespasian explained to him his schemes, for he was already then aiming at the supreme power. Apollonius encouraged him, and to his great surprise informed him that it was his destiny to rebuild the temple of Jupiter Capitolinus at Rome. As a matter of fact the temple had just been burned down, but the news did not reach Egypt till some time later. What we call nowadays a telepathic wave had conveyed the incident to the knowledge of the seer. A similar instance of Apollonius's telepathic powers is narrated in connection with the death of Domitian. Apollonius had previously been arrested by this Emperor on the ridiculous charge of sacrificing an Arcadian boy, in order, apparently, to discover the prospects of the succession of Nerva to the Empire. He was acquitted by the monster who was Nero's rival in cruelty without Nero's artistic talents, to the great surprise of all his friends. The story is that he vanished mysteriously from the court. We may, however, I think, without hesitation attribute this incident to Philostratus's love of the dramatic, especially as it seems clear that he had already been acquitted and that there was no apparent reason why he should not walk out as a free man like any ordinary mortal in similar circumstances. What strikes the dispassionate reader as really remarkable is the fact that though Apollonius was twice arrested, once by Nero and again by Domitian, and though the philosophers of the day, being supposed to be hostile to the tyrants, met almost invariably with short shrift, the sage of Tyana was in each case acquitted and left the court, as we say to-day, "without a stain on his character." Why, if the Emperors had him arrested, knowing doubtless the value of the charges against him, did they not take steps to ensure his condemnation? The fact seems to be, without doubt, that they regarded him with fear. Whether this fear was due merely to his reputation as a worker of wonders, or to his actual psychic power exercised at their expense in the courts of justice, is an open question, and clearly admits of two opinions.

His own observations on this subject, as quoted by Philostratus, seem, however, to justify our accepting by preference the latter of the two views. Speaking to his friends about his intention to take ship for Rome in order to meet openly any charge that might be made against him rather than to lie low in some distant corner of the Empire as his disciples were anxious that he should do, he observed that he would not consider a man a coward because he had disappeared out of dread of Nero, but would hail as a philosopher any one who rose superior to such a fear. And he added, " Let not any one think it foolish so to venture along a path which many philosophers are fleeing from, for in the first place I do not esteem any human agency so formidable that a wise man can ever be terrified by it, and in the second place I would not urge upon you the pursuit of bravery unless it were attended with danger." After dwelling upon the ferocity and brutality of Nero, contrasting him with savage animals who could sometimes be tamed, and mollified by coaxing and flattery, whereas Nero was only roused to greater cruelty than before by those who stroked him, he continued in the following remarkable strain :

If, however, any one is disposed to dread Nero for these reasons, and is led abruptly to forsake philosophy, conceiving that it is not safe for him to thwart his evil temper, let him know that the quality of inspiring fear really belongs to those who are devoted to temperance and wisdom, because they are sure of Divine succour. But let him snap his fingers at the threats of the proud and insolent, as he would at those of drunken men, for we regard these surely as daft and senseless, but not as formidable.

We are accustomed to refer to Apollonius as a philosopher. While we are perfectly correct in so doing, it is well to observe what the term philosophy connotes when employed by the Tyanian sage. It is not obviously a question merely of adopting a creed or view of life or a certain set of philosophical opinions, but implies in the fullest measure the life led in accordance with these opinions and inspired by the courage with which the knowledge of their truth endows the man who professes them. The keynote, indeed, to the whole of Apollonius's life lies in the fact that his so-called philosophy was an active and inspiring force which dominated his whole conduct.

I have alluded to the evidence of Apollonius's telepathic powers in connection with the death of Domitian. His passage of arms with this tyrant may have afforded the requisite psychic link. In any case the Tyanian was made aware of Domitian's assassination under sufficiently dramatic circumstances. He had returned to Ionia after a stay of two years in Greece, and was at the moment speaking at Ephesus. In the midst of his discourse he seemed to lose the current of his words, and the audience noticed a troubled expression passing over his features. Suddenly breaking off any further attempt to continue his speech, he stepped forward three or four paces on the platform from which he was addressing the assembly, and cried out in loud tones, " Strike the tyrant ! Strike ! " The audience were naturally amazed at this sudden outburst, but soon coming to himself, Apollonius explained to them that Domitian had been slain at that hour, and that a vision from the gods had been granted to him at the moment of what actually took place. News arrived in due course confirming his statement. This story is narrated by Dion Cassius as well as by Philostratus.

Beyond these records there are several others of a sufficiently startling character, which it is not easy to take too literally. There is, for instance, the narrative of the rescue of a young Athenian from the clutches of a vampire. The youth, according to the story, mistook the vampire for a normal living woman, and being infatuated with her, was on the point of marrying her until Apollonius dispelled the illusion. Probably this was one of the many romances that had collected round the name of Apollonius between his death and the time of Philostratus, though there may possibly have been some small grain of truth at the bottom of it. Another story which may have had some basis in fact, has been so embroidered upon as to render it quite incredible in the form in which it is presented by the biographer. This relates to the supposed interview of Apollonius with the ghost of Achilles, which was held to haunt the tomb of the Grecian hero. The reputation of Apollonius was so great and his supposed power as a worker of miracles had obtained so widespread a currency by the second century of our era that all sorts of miraculous happenings were readily credited by the ignorant public when ascribed to the Tyanian sage. Philostratus appears to have made use of certain of these floating stories.

That the name of Apollonius was regarded with the greatest veneration during the centuries following his death is abundantly evident. Caracalla (Roman Emperor 211–216 A.D.) honoured his memory with a chapel or monument (*heroum*).

APOLLONIUS OF TYANA

Alexander Severus (Emperor 225-235 A.D.) placed his statue in his *lararium* along with those of Christ, Abraham, and Orpheus. Aurelius is stated to have vowed a temple to the sage of Tyana, of whom he had seen a vision. Vopiscus at the end of the third century speaks of him as " a sage of the most widespread renown and authority, an ancient philosopher and a true friend of the gods." " He it was," says Vopiscus, " who gave life to the dead. He it was who did and said so many things beyond the power of men." In the work entitled *Quaestiones et Responsiones ad Orthodoxos*, attributed (though apparently in error) to Justin Martyr, occurs among other of these " questions " the following : " If God is the maker and master of creation how do the *telesmata* of Apollonius have power in the orders of that creation ? For as we see, they check the fury of the waves and the power of the winds, and the inroads of vermin and attacks of wild beasts." These *telesmata* or talismans were articles that had been, or were supposed to have been, consecrated or magnetised, with some religious ceremony, by Apollonius.[1]

We see, then, that around the name of this philosopher gathered, as time went on, a mass of more or less incredible miraculous tradition. And,

[1] I am indebted to G. R. S. Mead's work, *Apollonius of Tyana, The Philosopher-Reformer of the First Century A.D.* (London : T. P. S.), for these particulars.

as happens too often in such cases, the real work of this great religious reformer was lost sight of amid this accumulation of legend that impressed the popular eye, which was too dull to appreciate or understand the deeper significance of the life-work and esoteric teaching of the sage. Orthodox religion in the Roman Empire had indeed at this time fallen into very much the same sort of discredit as orthodox Christianity has among ourselves to-day. Two definite attempts were made to resuscitate these old religions of Greece and Rome by reviving the understanding of the essential spiritual truths which they enshrined ; the first by Apollonius of Tyana, who was above all else a reformer of the ancient Greek religion from within, and the other, an abortive one three hundred years later, by Julian the so-called Apostate. These classical faiths were, however, too much overlaid with mythological stories of an unedifying character ever again to recover their ascendancy over the popular imagination, and the ascetic life and esoteric interpretation which appealed to the isolated religious communities which Apollonius visited in his extensive travels throughout the countries bordering the Mediterranean, and as far east as Persia and India, could not in their very nature make a popular appeal to the average man. We see now that the triumph of Christianity was due to the universality of its appeal, and that however uncertain the issue of the struggle of the contending faiths appeared at the time, that issue was never really in doubt. The ascetic philosopher worked for the little public to whom the life of self-denial and esoteric truth are all in all, and to whom the world and the pursuits of the ordinary citizen take a place of minor importance. The "friend of publicans and sinners," "who was in all things tempted like as we are," was able to "draw all men unto him" by a compelling force such as the austere discipline and profound philosophy of Apollonius could never command. Jesus of Nazareth, in short, triumphed —and there is a profound significance in this fact— because mankind in the realisation of his true humanity forgot that he was accounted a God. The life of Apollonius was so far removed from anything the average man could comprehend that the world lost sight of the wisdom and deep spirituality of his teaching, in amazement at a worker of miracles so far beyond human ken that he came to be reckoned even a manifestation of Deity.

We are not, however, justified in supposing that it was primarily to his miracle-working powers that Apollonius owed his reputation among his contemporaries. It was rather as the wise man who had more knowledge and experience of the world than those around him, whose judgment was sounder and more unbiased by personal considerations than other men's, and whose high spirituality kept him aloof from all considerations of private gain or private interest, that Apollonius was regarded by the men of his own day. Later tradition which invested him with all kinds of miraculous achievements served to dim the halo round a great name. The foremost men of his time in thought and action, the Emperors Vespasian, Titus, and many others, did not come to consult Apollonius because he was some master magician. We do not in effect ask advice of a man in our hour of need because he can do the vanishing trick in a court of law, or pull rabbits out of his hat when there are no rabbits to pull, or do any of the marvellous performances which strike the vulgar with amazement. We seek rather the advice of one whose judgment is saner and whose knowledge of the world is greater than that of his fellows. It was for this reason that the wisest of the Roman Emperors came to consult Apollonius by preference with regard to the great task with which they were entrusted, when they had all the highest intellects in the Roman Empire from which to choose.

The account of Titus's first meeting with the Tyanian sage is of some interest, and not without its humorous side. Apollonius, who was already acquainted with his father, sent greetings to Titus, after the suppression of the Jewish insurrection, saying in characteristic manner, " Whereas you have refused to be proclaimed for success in war and for shedding the blood of your enemies, I myself assign to you the crown of temperance and moderation because you thoroughly understand what deeds really merit a crown." Titus thoroughly appreciated the compliment, and was not to be outdone by the other's courtesy. " On my own behalf," he replied, " I thank you no less than on behalf of my father, and I will not forget your kindness. For although I have captured Jerusalem, you have captured me."

After Titus had been appointed to share his father's responsibilities in the government of the Empire he did not forget Apollonius, and when he was in Tarsus wrote to the sage begging him to come and see him.

When he had arrived [says the narrative], Titus embraced him, saying, " My father has told me by letter everything in respect of which he consulted you ; and lo ! here is his letter, in which you are described as his benefactor and the being to whom we owe all that we are. Now though I am only just thirty years of age, I am held worthy of the same privileges to which my father only attained at the age of sixty. I am called to the throne to rule, perhaps before I have learnt myself to obey, and I therefore dread lest I am undertaking a task beyond my powers." Thereupon Apollonius, after stroking his neck, said (for he had as stout a neck as any athlete in training),

" And who will force so sturdy a bull-neck as yours under the yoke ? " " He that from my youth up reared me as a calf," answered Titus, meaning his own father, and implying that he could only be controlled by the latter, who had accustomed him from childhood to obey himself. " I am delighted then," said Apollonius, " in the first place, to see you prepared to subordinate yourself to your father, whom without being his natural children so many are delighted to obey, and next to see you rendering to his court homage in which others will associate yourself. When youth and age are paired in authority, is there any lyre or any flute that will produce so sweet a harmony and so nicely blended ? For the qualities of old age will be associated with those of youth, with the result that old age will gain in strength and youth in discipline."

The records of Apollonius's pithy sayings are very numerous and give a better insight into the man's character than the startling achievements with which he is so commonly credited. Once, when staying at Smyrna, he complimented the inhabitants on their zeal for letters and philosophy and their numerous activities, urging them to take pride rather in themselves than in the beauty of their city, for " although they had the most beautiful of cities under the sun, and although they had a friendly sea at their doors, nevertheless it was more pleasing for the city to be crowned with men than with porticoes and pictures, or even with gold in excess of what they needed." " For," he said, " public edifices remain where they are and are nowhere seen except in that particular part of the earth where they exist, but good men are conspicuous everywhere and everywhere talked about, and so they can magnify the city the more to which they belong in proportion to the numbers in which they are able to visit any part of the earth." And again, when visiting the monument to Leonidas, the hero of Thermopylæ, he was enthusiastic in admiration for the Greek leader, and on coming to the mound where the Lacedemonians were said to have been overwhelmed by the arrows which the enemy rained upon them, he heard his companions discussing with one another which was the loftiest peak in Hellas, the topic being suggested, apparently, by the sight of Mount Oeta which rose before their eyes. Accordingly ascending the mound, he said, "I consider this the loftiest of all, for those who fell here in defence of freedom raised it to a level with Oeta and carried it to a height surpassing many mountains like Olympus." On another occasion when, on arriving at Athens, and meeting with an enthusiastic reception at the hands of the people, he proposed to be initiated into the Eleusinian Mysteries, the hierophant showed jealousy of Apollonius's great reputation, which he felt put his own into the shade, and was reluctant, accordingly, to admit so formidable a rival. He therefore made the excuse that Apollonius was a wizard and had dabbled in impure rites, and that he could not in consequence consent to initiate him. Apollonius, however, was fully equal to the occasion, and retorted, "You have not yet mentioned the chief head of my offending, which is that knowing as I do more about the initiatory rite than you do yourself, I have nevertheless come for initiation to you as if you were wiser than I am." The attitude of the crowd was so hostile to the hierophant, on discovering his rejection of their honoured guest, that he found it advisable to change his tone. But Apollonius preferred to postpone his initiation till a later occasion, and, it is said, foretold the name of the successor who was destined to initiate him four years after.

Of many men who have led a deeply spiritual life and sacrificed everything for the sake of the pursuit of a spiritual ideal, it is recorded that they were wild and profligate in youth. Such was the case with St Francis of Assisi, and Apollonius's contemporary, the zealous Saul of Tarsus, led a changed life from the moment of his conversion. Indeed it has been said, referring doubtless to such instances, that "the greater the sinner the greater the saint." This saying, however, is by no means applicable to Apollonius. From his earliest days his choice was made clear. He came of a family which was at once wealthy and well-connected, and in addition to this he was endowed by nature with exceptional abilities and a remarkable memory, while the beauty of his person excited universal admiration. Every temptation, therefore, which fortune could offer, might, one would have thought, have led him to choose the path of worldly success. From the age of fourteen, however, he abandoned all idea of the pursuit of pleasure and devoted himself to discovering among the numerous Greek philosophies of the day some school of thought which would enable him to live up to his own ideals. Finally he adopted the system of Pythagoras, but was not content to receive it in the sense of accepting its doctrines and not living the life, after the manner of his teacher, Euxenus. Accordingly when Euxenus asked him how he would begin his new mode of life, he replied, " As doctors purge their patients." " Hence " (says G. R. S. Mead, in his Biography), " he refused to touch anything that had animal life in it, on the ground that it densified the mind and rendered it impure. He considered that the only pure form of food was what the earth produced, fruits and vegetables. He also abstained from wine, for, though it was made from fruit, it rendered turbid the ether in the soul, and destroyed the composure of the mind." In addition to this, he went barefoot, let his hair grow long, and wore nothing but linen.

On the death of his father, when he was twenty

years of age, he inherited a considerable fortune, which was left to him to share with his elder brother, a dissolute young man of three-and-twenty. When his brother had run through his share of the patrimony, he endeavoured (successfully as it appears) to rescue him from his vicious life, and made over to him half his own share of the inheritance. Having distributed the major part of the remainder among his relatives, he merely retained for himself a bare pittance.

Before starting on his missionary activities—he was probably by far the greatest traveller of his time—he took the vow of silence for five years. After this, he travelled from place to place making the acquaintance of temple priests and heads of the religious communities, endeavouring always to bring back the public cults to the purity of their ancient traditions and to suggest improvements in the practices of the private brotherhoods, the most important part of his work being devoted to those who were followers of the inner life. *Public* instruction in ethics and practical life he never gave until after the middle of the day, "for," he said, "those who live the inner life should on day's dawning enter the presence of the gods, spending the time till midday in giving and receiving instructions in holy things." His Indian expedition, from which his friends and disciples endeavoured to dissuade him, he undertook, as he stated, on the advice of his inner monitor, starting his perilous undertaking entirely alone, and so continuing until he made the acquaintance of Damis at Nineveh.

There is some doubt as to the date of Apollonius's birth, but an allusion by Philostratus makes it appear that he was quite a young man at the time of his Indian expedition, and as he apparently did not commence his five years' vow of silence till after he came of age, we must assume that he was somewhere between twenty-six and thirty at the commencement of this undertaking. Treadwell dates the Indian travels as from 41 to 54 A.D. If this is approximately accurate we may assign his birth-date to the second decade of the first century of the Christian era. Assuming this to be the case, he was presumably over eighty years old at the time of his death, which occurred about 98 A.D. Damis had been his almost inseparable companion from the time when he first met him at Nineveh. It seems to have been a case of something akin to "love at first sight," for the Assyrian was seized at once with an enthusiasm for the nobility of Apollonius's character, which was blent with a natural and even dog-like affection. At the last, however, his companion was not with him, and there is some mystery as to the exact place and occasion of his death. He sent Damis away when the expected time approached, on the pretext of entrusting him with a confidential letter to the Emperor Nerva, so that it may be said of him, as it was of Moses, " No man knoweth his burial place unto this day."

Apollonius had never reason to regret his Indian travels. He became deeply imbued with the metaphysical ideas of the Brahmins, and was in the habit ever after of extolling their spiritual philosophy as the fountain-head of all the profounder truths of Western religion. As to Damis's record of Apollonius's sojourn with the Indian Philosophers, we have only Philostratus's garbled account to guide us, and the quotation of Apollonius's cryptic observation, " I saw men dwelling on the earth and yet not on it ; defended on all sides, without any defence ; and yet possessed of nothing but what all possessed." It may be well to quote the interpretation of this saying given by Mr Mead. "They were on the earth but not of the earth, for their minds were set on things above. They were protected by their innate spiritual power, of which we have so many instances in Indian literature. And yet they possessed nothing but what all men possess if they would but develop the spiritual part of their being." There are a good many references in the conversations with Apollonius to the belief in Reincarnation, which was of course an essential tenet of Pythagorean philosophy, and he himself averred that in his previous life he was a man of no consequence, to wit, a ship's pilot. A letter ascribed to him, whether rightly or wrongly, has some interesting observations on this subject.

"Why has this false notion," he asks, "of birth and death" (*i.e.*, that they are real and not illusory in character)—"why has this false notion remained so long without being refuted? Some think that what has happened through them they have themselves brought about. They are ignorant that the individual is brought to birth *through* parents, not *by* parents. Just as a thing produced through the earth is not produced from it. The change which comes to the individual is nothing that is caused by his visible surroundings, but rather a change in the one thing which is in every man."

The portrait of Apollonius which has been handed down through many generations has become blurred and disfigured beyond recognition, and it seemed therefore well to give, even if in but a brief outline, such a sketch as might convey a juster idea of the philosopher whose friendship the greatest men of his day considered it their highest honour to enjoy, the man who chose the path of sanctity at a time of life when others choose "the primrose path of dalliance," who chose Wisdom for her own sake and Truth for the sake of Truth.

The world holds no record of a long life lived more nobly, of a more undaunted courage in confronting the tyrant, of a more unflinching tenacity of purpose, of a more single-minded devotion to a high ideal. His boyhood's choice, the inspiration of his manhood, the beacon-light of his latest years—to follow in the footsteps of that Form, so austere in the simplicity of her loveliness, " whose ways are ways of pleasantness and all whose paths are peace."[1]

[1] " Happy is the man that findeth wisdom. Length of days is in her right hand and in her left hand riches and honour. Her ways are ways of pleasantness and all her paths are peace " (Prov. iii. 13, 16, 17).

II

PLOTINUS

THE problem of the origin of the universe is one with which every religion in a certain sense claims to deal ; but it is a problem only of the most recondite sphere of metaphysics, while religions generally, in order to ensure their success, make appeal to popular sympathy and endeavour to bring down the truths which they enshrine to the intellectual level of the masses of mankind. To put abstruse truths into simple language is an impossibility. They can, however, be conveyed by a species of symbolism, or presented in an allegorical form which will be interpreted in one sense by the vulgar and in another by the philosopher or the religious initiate. The communication of these hidden truths has been represented in the case of most religions as a definite revelation from a higher plane ; but whatever claim is made as to their origin, they are at least put before the rank and file of the faithful as dogmas to be accepted unhesitatingly as a vital element of the orthodox religion of the time or country. Such dogmas in their crude form, it is needless to say, have never made appeal to the high philosophical intelligence of the day. Under the autocratic regime of persecuting Christianity during the Middle Ages of Europe, Christian dogma was indeed accepted nominally by great intellects, but it was accepted under duress and with a reservation, and subject to such interpretations of its inner meaning as might commend themselves to the mental standpoint of their professor. The men of highest intellect were compelled to express the faith that was in them in the most guarded language, and if they failed to do so they were only too liable to share the fate of Galileo, or—worse still—of Giordano Bruno. The sole exception to this rule is to be found in Oriental countries, such as India, where religion, whether Brahmin or Buddhist, has assumed a less dogmatic form, and has found it possible accordingly to assimilate and identify itself with philosophical speculations of the profoundest and most abstruse character, without any sense of incongruity or doing violence to its own specific tenets. It is true that Mohammedanism appears to contradict this, but it must be remembered that the religion of Mohammed was in the nature of a foreign importation and not indigenous to Indian soil.

Thus it came about that the philosophers of

PLOTINUS

early Greece and Rome were almost invariably avowed sceptics as regards the popular religious beliefs of their time, though in spite of this, with the sole exception of Socrates, they were allowed to preach their doctrines openly in the market place without let or hindrance. Thus, too, the triumph of Christianity brought it eventually into open antagonism with philosophic thought. In this case, however, the dogmatic and intolerant character of the creed suffered no rival schools of opinion, and accordingly, within 200 years of the date at which it was established by Constantine as the recognised religion of the Roman Empire, the Athenian schools of philosophy were forcibly suppressed by Justinian.[1] For some two and a half centuries before this latter date Neoplatonism in one form or another had dominated the intellectual world of philosophy. It had superseded the materialistic philosophies of earlier Rome and Greece, and even before the time of Constantine, the Stoic and Epicurean schools of thought had already ceased to appeal to the inquiring spirit of the time. When, after a thousand years of intervening barbarism, under the influence of the Renaissance movement, men began to turn their attention once more to classic scholarship and classic philosophy, it was to Plato, mainly as interpreted

[1] Constantine became sole Emperor in 323 A.D. The Athenian schools of philosophy were suppressed by Justinian in 529 A.D.

by his successor and follower, Plotinus, that the leading spirits of the day turned in search of a solution of those problems of life which were once more pressing for interpretation, after the intellectual death in life of the Dark Ages, following the break-up of the Roman Empire. Christianity, indeed, had its metaphysics—for every religion is bound, in a sense, to explain its Divinity to its devotees—but they were the bastard metaphysics of the Athanasian Creed, the expression of a political compromise drawn up to satisfy the warring sects of Christendom. Far different was the effort of Plotinus, who sought not only to solve the riddle of the sphinx, but to express in language intelligible to his hearers the solution of the profoundest mysteries of the universe. How far he succeeded in doing so is yet in dispute to the present day. At least the basis of his philosophy still remains as an attempted approximation to the truth which forms the groundwork for the efforts of every new seeker after spiritual enlightenment.

At the date of the birth of Plotinus, Alexandria was the intellectual capital of the world. There met East and West, in spite of Mr Rudyard Kipling's dictum to the contrary. There the philosophical and intellectual speculations of the entire civilised world enjoyed a common forum where the most diverse views found a ready audience.

There Philo interpreted Judaism in terms of current Greek thought. There Gnostics and Christians contended for the supremacy of their various religious doctrines. There, among others, Ammonius Saccas lectured on his philosophical interpretation of the universal life, first from a standpoint akin to that of the new Christian religion, which was already obtaining so many converts, and later from an independent platform of his own. To him, after listening to many different philosophers, in whose views he found neither satisfaction nor illumination, came the most illustrious of his pupils, Plotinus. Plotinus was at this time about twenty-eight (he was born probably at Lycopolis in Egypt, in the year 205 or 206 A.D.), and he continued to remain at Alexandria and to elaborate his theories under the auspices of his master, Ammonius, for some eleven years. At the expiration of this period the similarity of the philosophy of Ammonius to that taught by the Brahmins of India, and doubtless also the interest in these Oriental conceptions which had been stimulated by the travels of Apollonius of Tyana, led to a decision on the part of Plotinus to emulate the Tyanian sage and himself embark on a similar mission. The expedition of the Emperor Gordian against the Persians appeared to supply a favourable opportunity for carrying out this project. This expedition was, however, destined to disaster, and Gordian met with an untimely end. Plotinus himself barely escaped with his life, but eventually reached Antioch in safety. Our philosopher did not remain long in the Syrian capital, but at the earliest opportunity sailed for Rome, where the remainder of his life was spent in lecturing and in philosophic study and discussion.

It was not until he had lived in Rome for ten years that, at the urgent request of his followers, he commenced writing what subsequently became known as *The Enneads of Plotinus*. Twenty-one of these books were completed when, at the age of fifty-nine, he first met Porphyry, who is our principal source of information with regard to his manner of life and the main facts of his career. To Porphyry was eventually allotted the task of editing his writings, which he divided into six volumes of nine books each, the number of books in each volume being thus used to give a name to his whole system of philosophy (Enneads, Greek ἐννεα, nine).

That his treatises were in urgent need of a competent editor is apparent from the observations which Porphyry makes with regard to his methods of composition. He was in the habit of writing down his thoughts just as they occurred to him, and " could not (says his biographer) by any means endure to review twice what he had written, nor

PLOTINUS

even to read his own composition," mainly on account of his defective eyesight. Nor, indeed, was he by any means a perfect master of the Greek language, in which his lectures were delivered and his books written. Porphyry in fact observes, let us hope with some exaggeration, that he "neither formed the letters with accuracy, nor exactly distinguished the syllables, nor bestowed any diligent attention on the orthography, but neglecting all these as trifles, he was alone attentive to the intellection of his wonderful mind, and, to the admiration of all his disciples, persevered in this custom to the end of his life."

One is, indeed, not a little impressed how entirely, in the later days of the Roman Empire, "captive Greece led captive her conquerors." Greek philosophy and Greek ideas had, in truth, permeated the whole civilised world. Not only was this the case, but when the Western or Roman Empire fell eventually into decrepitude and ruin, its Eastern partner, though threatened and harassed by barbarian foes on all its borders, continued to survive the extinction of the erstwhile mistress of the world by something like a thousand years. Alexandria was, however, destined to destruction by an Arab invasion long ere this, and never recovered from its sack by the Mohammedan Amru in A.D. 640. The survival of the Eastern Empire was doubtless due in great part to the superior vitality of the Greek race ; but it does not admit of doubt that it would have fallen a victim to the Moslem invader at least 500 years before the date of its final doom, had it not been for Constantine's choice of an Eastern capital and the almost impregnable position enjoyed by the imperial city. It is open to conjecture that had the British Government of the present day been better acquainted with the history of Constantinople and the many sieges which it had successfully sustained, they would have thought twice, and indeed thrice, before launching without adequate preparation, the ill-fated expedition to the Dardanelles.

The dialectical disquisitions of Plotinus were delivered in Greek, and his whole trend of thought was essentially Greek in character. One is inclined to ask oneself indeed whether the Latin language would have been capable of expressing the subtleties of his philosophical speculation. In this connection the similarity of his ideas to those enunciated in the great Vedantic system of Indian philosophy must not blind us to the fact that his method of treating his subject, and the closely reasoned arguments which he adduces in the defence of his scheme of the universe, are purely and entirely Greek. This appears to me to be the real truth in relation to a much disputed point, as to what

Plotinus owed to Indian thought on the one hand, and to Greek culture and Greek philosophy on the other. When Milton appealed to the Divine Muse to enable him to "soar above the Aonian Mount" and achieve "things unattempted yet in prose or rhyme," he was in truth taking on a small order compared with the tremendous task which Plotinus set himself in his attempted solution of the riddle of the universe. To say that his exposition of his system lends itself to criticism in more than one vital point is merely to state that he was human. Whoever attempts to go behind phenomena and postulate a First Cause, whether we denominate that Cause The One, like Plotinus, or The Good, like Plato, or The Absolute, like Herbert Spencer, is manifestly passing into realms of thought with which the human mind is incompetent to deal. It stands to reason, indeed, that the finite mind cannot comprehend the infinite, and logic, therefore, inevitably fails us. But there is in truth another side to this most recondite problem. Though logic cannot fathom it, and though the finite cannot comprehend the infinite, yet the infinite spirit may contact infinity. In other words, the infinite in man, that is, the divine spark, which is part and parcel of infinity, may realise the infinite within itself, not, indeed, by any logical process, but by the immediate experience implicit in spiritual union. Hence the possibility of that form of mystical ecstasy which has been denominated Cosmic Consciousness, and which it is narrated that Plotinus experienced no less than four times during the six years, 262-268, when Porphyry was his companion in Rome. The effect of these experiences on Plotinus is very evident in his philosophy. They led to his emphasising the unity of all creation, and its oneness with the Divine, and the natural corollary of this, the illusory nature of separate individuality. Hence that which causes individuality, the principle of limitation inherent in matter, appears to him itself also of an illusory nature, that is, essentially incapable of acquiring or participating in real existence. From this negative character of matter arise, according to Plotinus, the imperfections of the material universe, and its inability to conform to the ideal or intelligible order.

At the basis of the system of Plotinus there is postulated then an ideal universe which constitutes an archetype or pattern of the phenomenal order which our senses apprehend. Plotinus assumes three root principles which he denominates the Three Divine Hypostases, and which have been since designated the Alexandrian Trinity, though it would be a mistake to confuse this triad with the Trinity of the Christian Creed. The First Divine Hypostasis is the Prime Source of Being, denominated, as already stated, the One or the Good. This corresponds to the Absolute of the Spencerian philosophy, and Plotinus tells us that it transcends all known attributes—so much so, in fact, that even existence itself cannot be predicated of it. Every being, according to the Plotinian system, tends to produce an image of itself. Hence we have the Second and Third of these Divine Principles, emanating in their turn from the First. The Second Divine Hypostasis our philosopher designates the Intelligible Universe or Universal Intelligence. This is the sphere of Absolute Reality or Essence, and constitutes a manifestation of the creative power of the One. The Third Divine Hypostasis is the Universal Soul, and this again is the image of the Second; but it differs from its principal in the fact that life in its sphere is no longer inert or motionless, but revolves about and within the Universal Intelligence. By way of explanation, Plotinus offers the parallel of one circle enclosed within another and larger but concentric circle which revolves about it, the common centre of both being represented by the One or First Hypostasis, the motionless inner circle by the Universal Intelligence, and the revolving outer circle by the Universal Soul; though it is recognised that this form of symbolism can be pressed too far, as the expressions "external" and "internal" in this connection have no real validity.

Matter, as already stated, is regarded as possessing no definite attributes of its own ; but it is capable of receiving a semblance of life by reflecting the forms derived by the Universal Soul from the Second Divine Principle or Intelligible Universe. Matter, then, serves as a mirror upon which the Universal Soul projects the images or reflections of its creations, and thus gives rise to the phenomena of the sensible universe. This universe, which we are accustomed to term the Phenomenal World, holds an intermediate position between Reality and Negation owing to its participation in matter, which Plotinus identifies with Evil as being the negation of the Spiritual or Real. The existence of the Universal Soul is an eternal contemplation of the One as revealed in the sphere of Intelligence or Beauty (the Second Divine Hypostasis) and is itself an indivisible noncorporeal essence, possessing omnipresent consciousness. While, then, one part of the Universal Soul inhabits the sphere of Intelligence, its inferior part has relation with the Sensible World, or Material Universe. The Universal Soul by this relation with the Material Universe gives birth to the phenomena of Nature in all their varied manifestation. But whereas the object of contemplation of the Universal Soul is the One as revealed in terms of Beauty or the Intelligible Order, the object of the contemplation of Nature is Nature itself. Nature, in short, contemplates the forms of its own creation, and hence arise the imperfections of its manifestation.

"The character of the material universe [following Dr Whitby,[1] in his summary of the doctrine of Plotinus] is thus due to the irradiation of matter or chaos by the complex unity of forms or reasons (*logoi*) derived by the Universal Soul from its contemplation of the sphere of essential reality and Absolute Perfection. By reason of the inability of matter to participate fully in the real qualities of existence, it follows that the perfection of the material universe is inferior to that of the Universal Soul, and still more so to that of the Intelligible Universe." In writing "on the nature and origin of evil," our philosopher observes, "Whatever is deficient of good in a small degree is not yet evil, since it is capable from its nature of becoming perfect. But whatever is perfectly destitute of good, and such is matter, is evil in reality, possessing no portion of good. For, indeed, matter does not,

[1] To whose book, *The Wisdom of Plotinus* (Rider, 3s. 6d. net) I must acknowledge my indebtedness.

properly speaking, possess being, by means of which it might be invested with good. But the attribute of being is only equivocally affirmed of matter."

The association of matter with the soul arises from the voluntary determination of the individual consciousness towards the material plane. But it must not be supposed that this commingling of the soul and matter results in any actual union between the two in the same sense as in the chemical world hydrogen and oxygen combine to form water. For matter, as explained above, is in the nature of a mirror which the divine light of the soul illuminates but which is incapable of receiving into itself that light by which it is illuminated. " But [observes Plotinus][1] matter obscures by its sordid mixture and renders feeble the light which emanates from the soul and, by opposing the waters of generation, it occasions the soul's entrance into the rapid stream, and by this means renders her light, which is in itself vigorous and pure, polluted and feeble, like the faint glimmerings from a watch tower beheld in a storm. For if matter were never present, the soul would never approach to generation ; and this is the lapse of the soul, thus to descend into matter and become debilitated and impure,

[1] Plotinus on *The Nature and Origin of Evil* (Taylor's Translation).

inasmuch as matter prohibits many of the soul's powers from their natural activities, comprehending and as it were contracting the place which the soul contains, in her dark embrace." Matter thus is the cause of the evil inherent in the material world, as without this the soul would have for ever remained " permanent and pure."

Matter, in itself, possesses no form, being unable to sustain order or measure. The soul, however, by its union with matter, imposes form upon it, this form being the result of the combination of the limitation inherent in matter, in union with the archetypal idea of which the soul is the expression. We have, then, a conception of the universe, of which the One represents Infinity, and matter, the opposite pole, or zero. Owing, however, to the fact that no attributes or qualities can be predicated of the One, and that this is, in a negative sense, also the case with matter, which is the privation of being, we arrive at a certain confusion, the attempts of our philosopher to explain matter leading to phrases which are equally applicable to Infinity or the One. The two extremes of Absolute Being and Non-Being appear, in short, to meet, and a resulting bewilderment arises in the mind, which one is rather inclined to gather, was not entirely absent from the thought of Plotinus himself. It may be suggested, tentatively, that this *impasse* arises rather from the failure of Plotinus to describe the One in more positive terms, than in his defective description of the negative qualities of matter. The fact that the One of Plotinus is conceived of as such that no language is able to express it, does not, in reality, justify the philosopher in describing it in terms of negation, however much positive statements may fall short of portraying the Absolute Reality. Of matter itself, however, we ought perhaps to predicate a relative though inferior reality; even while we admit that the presence of spirit is in inverse proportion to the density of matter.

In the view of Plotinus the universe is a single vast conscious organism of which all the parts are similarly endowed with consciousness. He attributes a species of divinity to the Sun and the stars, and appears to accept the theory of planetary spirits. Thus also Origen observes: "As our body while consisting of human members is yet held together by one soul, so the universe is to be thought of as an immense living being which is held together by one soul, the power of the logos, God."

According to Plotinus it is truer to state that the body is in the soul than that the soul is in the body, inasmuch as the soul is transcendent as well as immanent in the corporeal form. Thus, when a particular body acquires life the soul which is destined to animate it does not in reality descend into it and become identified with it, but rather the body comes within the sphere of its influence, thus attaining to the world of life. This explanation is, it seems to me, helpful in enabling us to understand the gradual process by which the individual consciousness becomes *en rapport* with the immature bodies of childhood. Following out the same theory we can understand the doctrine of early Gnostic sects, that Jesus of Nazareth was overshadowed by the Christ, and also we may believe, if we will, that the guardian angels of the little children who, as Jesus asserted, " do always behold the face of My Father which is in Heaven " are indeed their own higher spiritual selves, attracted on the one hand to those physical bodies of which they are the prospective tenants, and on the other looking regretfully back to their pre-natal home in the spiritual world.

Like the Deity, the soul is in the nature of a trinity, the occult axiom, " As above, so below " being implicit in Plotinus's philosophy. Thus man consists, firstly, of the animal, or sensual soul, which is closely united with the body; secondly, of the logical, or reasoning soul; and thirdly, of that individualised portion of the divine essence whose proper habitation is the Intelligible Universe, of which it in its origin forms a part. The return of the soul to the One is accomplished by means of a gradual process of purification, which eventually, after an immeasurable period of time, releases the soul from its inclination towards the plane of sensibility; *i.e.* its attraction to the material world. The philosophy of Plotinus thus included the doctrine of metempsychosis, as regards the affirmation of the truth of which he is very emphatic. For he declares that "The gods bestow on each the destiny which appertains to him, and which harmonises with his antecedents in his successive existences. Every one who is not aware of this is grossly ignorant of divine matters." He would even appear to admit that at times fallen human souls are imprisoned in the bodies of animals, but speaks less confidently on this head.

The conceptions of Plotinus explain many of those psychical phenomena which have so much puzzled our modern scientists, and offer a solution for the much-debated problems involved in the phenomena of telepathy, magic, and planetary influence. "The sensitivity of nature [writes Dr Whitby, summarising this side of Plotinus's philosophy] is manifested as a vital nexus in virtue of which every minutest and remotest particle of the universe is intimately correlated and symbolically united to the rest. The universe as a whole, al hough thus endowed with a potential sensitivity, may nevertheless be considered as impassive, because the soul which animates and pervades it has no need of sensations for its own enlightenment and does not, in fact, regard them. Nevertheless, and for the simple reason that nature is a living organism, sympathetic throughout, individual parts of the universe have a quasi-sensitivity, and respond to impressions from without. When, for example, the stars, in answer to human invocations, confer benefits upon men, they do so, not by a voluntary action, but because their natural or unreasoning psychical faculties are unconsciously affected. Similarly demons may be charmed by spells or prayers acting upon the unreasoning part of their nature." For, according to Plotinus, the universe is a vast chain, of which every being is a link.

Plotinus, like every one else who has attempted to solve the Riddle of the Sphinx, is up against the basic facts of existence. Boldly and perseveringly as we may attempt to face the problem, the Sphinx sits and smiles with the smile that will not come off, well knowing that however near we may seem to be to the solution of the mystery, the problem will still baffle us, and remain unsolved to the end. We may postulate a Deity who is all Perfection, but, if we do so, it rests with us to explain how it is that evil is present in the universe, if this Deity is in reality, as Plotinus and other philosophers have taught us, the All. We may postulate matter as inherently evil in nature, in opposition to the Good, but if so, whence comes that which is not included in the All ? If matter is the mere privation of good, whence come its apparently very positive qualities ? If the All is complete and perfect in itself, what need for the manifested universe ? What need for the striving after a higher perfection, which gives the lie to the Absolute Perfection predicated of the One ? Matthew Arnold has adopted the hypothesis of a " Power, not ourselves, which makes for righteousness " ; but in this hypothesis he first abandons the conception of the unity of the All and subsequently throws over the idea of divine perfection. For his Deity is, after all, only striving after a perfection which he has not yet reached.

The dualistic conception offers in truth fewer difficulties to the ordinary mind. It is more in accordance with the obvious facts of existence, which are brought under our notice every day of our lives. Deceptive and illusory though the conception may be, we still appear to be confronted by the existence of a gigantic struggle between good and evil in which the two combatants are more nearly matched than we care to admit. We like to shut our eyes to this and postulate a Deity of infinite power and infinite beneficence, but, while we do so, we are for ever admitting into our intellectual sphere certain conceptions that run counter to this theory, and in order to acquit our Deity of responsibility for the evil which we see ever around us, we make of the Devil a scapegoat who, in practice, bears on his shoulders the sins of the whole world ; or alternatively we accept a conception of God and the Devil which runs on parallel lines with that of Dickens' Spenlow and Jawkins. If behind Good and Evil, the two forces which are everlastingly struggling for the mastery, we have, as Plotinus and other of the wisest philosophers assure us, some principle of Unity from which both alike flow, are we justified in postulating of that Unity Absolute Perfection and Absolute Power ? Or are we not nearer the mark in describing it in the Nietzschean phrase as " beyond good and evil," as possessed of attributes and qualities which finite brains are incapable of apprehending ? Are we not indeed darkening counsel by attributing to this Unknown a perfection which, after all, the entire gamut of existence suggests to us has never yet been reached through all the æons even though we may be approaching nearer to it every day and every hour ?

The creation of the universe, if we are to accept the system of Plotinus, did not actually take place in time. He argues this point out with much subtlety and ingenuity in his essay "on Providence," rejecting the hypothesis of " a certain foresight and discursive consideration on the part of Deity, deliberating in what condition the world should be especially formed, and by what means it may be constituted as far as possible for the best "; and accepting in place of it the assumption that the universe always had a being, and that it was " formed according to intellect, and intellect not preceding *in time* but prior [1]; because the world is its offspring, and because intellect is the cause and the world its image, perpetually subsisting in the same manner and flowing from this as its source." In other words, being faced with the alternative of assuming a definite date at which life began, or postulating existence from all eternity, he accepts the latter as presenting the lesser difficulty of the two ; but in order to do so, he finds himself involved in the necessity of admitting a sequence of cause and effect which the finite mind is quite unable to dissociate from the conception of time. Failing this, his whole theory of the three Divine Hypostases falls to the ground. If we adopt the alternative which Plotinus rejected, we are plunged into still greater embarrassment ; for if creation began in time, why did the All or the One wait through all the æons of eternity [2] for its commencement ? And

[1] *I.e.*, prior in the sense that cause precedes effect.
[2] The Indian conception of the inbreathing and outbreathing of Brahma may help us here, but it does not entirely get over the difficulty.

PLOTINUS

how, indeed, did time itself evolve from eternity, in view of the fact that the two ideas have no apparent relation to each other ? The philosopher may

> . . . plunge into eternity where recorded time
> Seems but a point, and the reluctant mind
> Flags wearily in its unending flight
> Till it sink dizzy, blind, lost, shelterless.[1]

He may do this, indeed, but after all he will not have solved the Riddle of the Sphinx.

[1] Shelley, " Prometheus Unbound."

III

MICHAEL SCOT

THE name of Michael Scot is principally familiar to English readers through Sir Walter Scott's *Lay of the Last Minstrel*. Shakespeare's *Tempest* and Scott's *Lay of the Last Minstrel* are probably the two best-known works among English classics which breathe throughout the weird and fascinating atmosphere of mediæval magic. Prospero is a magician, and the whole plot of the *Tempest* is based upon his magical practices and their consequences. The Lady of Branksome in the *Lay of the Last Minstrel* has also learned from her father the "forbidden art."

>Her father was a clerk of fame
>   Of Bethune's line of Picardie :
>He learned the art that none may name,
>   In Padua, far beyond the sea.
>Men said, he changed his mortal frame
>   By feat of magic mystery ;
>For when, in studious mood, he paced
>   St Andrew's cloistered hall,
>His form no darkening shadow traced
>   Upon the sunny wall !
>And of his skill, as bards avow,
>   He taught that Ladye fair,
>Till to her bidding she could bow
>   The viewless forms of air.

In order the more effectually to accomplish her purposes, she dispatches her staunch henchman, William of Deloraine, to Melrose Abbey, where lies buried the wizard, Michael Scot, and buried with him, the Book of Might, which contains those potent spells whereby the great wizard had achieved his world-wide celebrity. "The Monk of St Mary's Aisle," now an ecclesiastical veteran of some hundred summers, had in earlier days fought the Moslem on the fields of Spain, and had there met and become an intimate friend of the much dreaded wizard. He had attended him at his deathbed, and had himself buried him in Melrose Abbey, receiving injunctions from him in his last hours never to allow the Book of Might to be disinterred "save at his chief of Branksome's need." For Michael Scot himself was a native of Teviot Dale, though his life had been spent in Italy, in Spain, and at Palermo in Sicily in attendance at the court of the Emperor Frederick II., whose fame became in a curious way linked with his own. The date of Michael Scot's departure from Sicily for Spain was approximately 1210 A.D., and coincided with the turning-point of that long war of centuries which ended in the ejection of the Moorish conquerors from the Spanish peninsula. 1212 A.D. was the date of the decisive battle of Las Navas, which resulted in a crushing defeat for the Moorish forces, and led within fifty years to their retirement from all parts of Spain with the exception of the province of Granada. Scot was at this time in Spain pursuing his studies in Alchemy, Astrology, and the forbidden arts generally, and translating the works of the learned Arabians, Avicenna, Averroes, and Geber, and rewriting their paraphrases of Aristotle in the Latin tongue, which was then the universal medium for the dissemination of all scientific and philosophic knowledge throughout Europe.

We may imagine the monk of St Mary's Aisle in his early days fighting the Moorish hosts in Spain and engaged, perhaps, in the great battle of Las Navas, which sealed their doom. Here he is represented by the poet as striking up a firm friendship with the student and philosopher, Michael Scot, and learning from him the secret of his magical practices. The monk is represented as telling William of Deloraine :

" In those far climes it was my lot
To meet the wondrous Michael Scot,
A wizard, of such dreaded fame,
That when, in Salamanca's cave,
Him listed his magic wand to wave,
The bells would ring in Notre Dame !
Some of his skill he taught to me ;
And, Warrior, I could say to thee
The words that cleft Eildon hills in three.

MICHAEL SCOT

And bridled the Tweed with a curb of stone :
But to speak them were a deadly sin ;
And for having but thought them my heart within,
A treble penance must be done."

These achievements, according to the legend, were attributed to Michael Scot's " familiar," to whom he entrusted first one task and then another, but finding his energies too tireless, and fearing he might engage in some mischief which would react detrimentally on himself, finally sent him to spin ropes of sand at the mouth of the Tweed. This operation being an unending one, is said to be still in progress, and as his biographer relates, the successive attempts and failures of the spirit are pointed out as every tide casts up or, receding, uncovers the ever-shifting sands of Berwick bar. The reference to bridling the Tweed with a curb of stone, is an allusion to the basaltic dyke which crosses the bed of the river near Ednam. Michael, according to the tale, enjoyed that complete mastery of words of power which in the traditions of ancient magic is so potent a force in the working of wonders. As the monk records in his conversation with the knight of Branksome :

" The words may not again be said
That he spoke to me, on death-bed laid ;
They would rend this Abbaye's massy nave
And pile it in heaps above his grave."

The monk was not unnaturally alarmed at the power that this archworker of spells might have given to the fiends of darkness, and took precaution to bury him

> . . . On St Michael's night,
> When the bell tolled one, and the moon was bright,

so that the cross of his patron saint reflected by the light of the moon from the emblazoned window pane might fall on the spot which was chosen for his grave. Once again on this fateful night the Red Cross was reflected on the sepulchral stone, and the opportunity which this offered to take possession of the Book of Might undisturbed by the hosts of darkness, must be taken without delay. Within the grave was one of those ever-burning lamps, for the existence of which there seems to be some historical evidence, and which was to serve in the present instance as a further protection for the wizard against the fiends of night. Deloraine's task achieved " by dint of passing strength " with the aid of a bar of iron handed him by the monk, the light

> Streamed upward to the chancel roof
> And through the galleries far aloof.
> No earthly flame blazed e'er so bright;
> It shone like Heaven's own blessed light.
> Before their eyes the Wizard lay
> As if he had not been dead a day,

MICHAEL SCOT

His hoary beard in silver roll'd,
He seem'd some seventy winters old ;
A palmer's amice wrapp'd him round,
With a wrought Spanish baldric bound,
  Like a pilgrim from beyond the sea :
His left hand held his Book of Might ;
A silver cross was in his right ;
  The lamp was placed beside his knee.
High and majestic was his look,
At which the fellest fiends had shook,
And all unruffled was his face ;
They trusted his soul had gotten grace.

William of Deloraine hesitated to perform what seemed very like an act of sacrilege. He was used to battlefields, but panic seized him in this strange scene, and the monk was eventually compelled to warn him that delay in such circumstances was dangerous.

" Now speed thee what thou hast to do,
  Or, warrior, we may dearly rue ;
For those thou may'st not look upon
Are gathering fast round the yawning stone ! "
Then Deloraine, in terror, took
From the cold hand the Mighty Book,
With iron clasped and with iron bound :
He thought, as he took it, the dead man frowned ;
But the glare of the sepulchral light,
Perchance, had dazzled the warrior's sight.

How the knight and priest withdrew from the chapel after the tombstone had been replaced, in the redoubled gloom of the night, " with wavering steps and with dizzy brain," imagining the walls of the chapel echoing with fiendish laughter as they retreated, is recounted dramatically enough by the bard of the Scottish border. We are, perhaps, more interested to know what manner of man this Michael Scot was, and how far these records of his magical powers are based on anything more than unauthenticated tradition. The facts we possess with regard to Michael Scot's career convince us indeed that he was a man of the greatest erudition and learning, and far in advance of his contemporaries in these respects. He was a noted mathematician, and not content with gaining the highest honours in the schools of Paris of that day, he subsequently pursued his studies at the fountainhead of mathematical and alchemical research at Toledo in Spain. For it must be remembered that we owe the basis of our mathematical knowledge primarily to the Arabs who introduced to Europe not only the Arabic numerals in place of the cumbrous Roman figures, but also the study of Algebra, itself an Arabic word. To the Arabs, too, we owe the basis of our Chemistry—a word that is, of course, synonymous with Alchemy, which again bears the stamp of its Arabian origin. It is curious indeed to note how far the civilisation of the Arab was in advance of that of the greater part of Europe in those days. Five hundred years before Michael

Scot took ship from Sicily for Spain, the Arabs had advanced across the whole of Northern Africa, conquering Egypt, Tripoli, Algeria, and Morocco in turn, and finally crossing to Spain and there establishing a separate kaliphate in the eighth century of the Christian era. The invasion of Spain by the Arabs introduced into the Iberian peninsula a literary culture of a kind till then quite unknown. Under the sway of the Moorish sovereigns the arts and architecture flourished, and science found a welcome which it met with nowhere else in Christianised Europe.

It was to the Moorish capital that students of the medical art repaired who desired to master the latest discoveries and most modern methods in the treatment of the human body. Irrigation with the Moors had become an applied science, and was employed extensively throughout the Iberian peninsula with the most advantageous results in enhancing the fertility of the soil. Nowhere else in Europe did the land yield such rich harvests, and nowhere else was the science of agriculture so fully understood. The fertile fields of those days are in many cases replaced by barren deserts and the towns with teeming populations by ruins and uninhabited wastes. The ignorant peasantry that has taken the place of the cultivated sons of Arabia are still in the matter of civilisation and commercial activity hundreds of years behind the busy and intelligent population whom in the latter part of the fifteenth century they finally drove over the seas after subjecting them to the most cruel persecution for adhering to the faith of their fathers. Three million Moors are said to have been ejected from Spanish soil at the bidding of the civil power, instigated by ecclesiastical tyranny. Civilisation has not yet rallied from the so-called " triumph of the Cross " in Spain. This ejection of the Moors from the west of Europe coincided, as it happened, with the advent of the Turk at Constantinople ; but here, by a curious contradiction, the Turk as the champion of Mohammedanism represented not progress but the triumph of the sword. The case was inverted, but in each instance it represented the victory of barbarism over civilisation, whether the Mohammedan made headway in the east or the Christian in the west. In the east the effete remnant of the Eastern Empire was swept away before the advancing hosts of Islam. In the west a far more highly developed and industrial population was wiped out at the bidding of the myrmidons of the Papal See.

For five hundred years the Moors had ruled all but the northernmost portion of Spain, and for another 250 they retained the province of Granada. Countless examples of their ornate and characteristic semi-oriental architecture remain behind as a record of their artistic culture, and much also of their language intermingled with that of the race which they at first conquered and which in the days of their luxury and decadence reconquered them in turn. But the intellectual life of Moorish Spain, which was for so long like a beacon light in the darkness of Mediæval Europe, has passed, never to return. The Inquisition marked the high-water mark of the reaction of Christian bigotry against the tolerant and broad-minded intellectuality which had flourished under the fostering dominion of a race whose glories to-day are but a memory of the far-distant past.

Scot as a mathematician, alchemist, and astrologer, had this been his sole life's work, would have merited no insignificant niche in the temple of Science ; but in addition to this, he exercised, though in an entirely indirect manner, a marked influence on the history of Europe. His talents and learning commended him for the position of tutor to Frederick II., at that time king only of Sicily, but afterwards " Emperor of the Romans." Frederick was an orphan, having lost both his parents in early childhood, and the receptive mind of the ardent boy responded sympathetically to the instructions of his broad-minded and accomplished tutor, who was destined subsequently to become his confidant and friend.

Michael Scot's first efforts as an author had for their aim the education of his royal pupil. For this purpose he first wrote the *Liber Introductorius*, and afterwards the *Liber Particularis* and the *Physionomia*. The first two of these books dealt with astronomy and astrology, and the latter with physiognomy and the reading of character from the physical appearance.

Marriages were arranged early in those days, and Frederick, when a boy of but fourteen, was united in wedlock, at the Pope's desire, with Constance, daughter of the King of Aragon, and widow of the King of Hungary, who was some ten years his senior. This brought the attendance of Michael Scot at the court at Palermo, temporarily at least, to an end, and led to his setting sail, as already narrated, for the coasts of Spain. It appears that the *Physionomia* was his parting gift on his marriage to his illustrious pupil. On his arrival in Spain, Scot betook himself to the headquarters of the scientific activities of those days, the renowned city of Toledo. Here, towards the middle of the twelfth century, a regular school for translations from the Arabic had been established, and it was work of this kind on which Scot himself embarked. Here he translated the *Abbreviatio Avicennæ* with a dedication to the Emperor Frederick in the following terms: " O ! Frederick, Lord of the World,

MICHAEL SCOT

and Emperor, receive with devotion this book of Michael Scot, that it may be a grace unto thy head and a chain about thy neck "—no empty compliment as such phrases generally are, nor one unappreciated by its distinguished recipient. Here, too, he pursued his studies in alchemy, chemistry, medicine, and astrology. Alchemy in those days was a special bone of contention, one school maintaining its feasibility, and the other denouncing it, after the manner of nineteenth century scientists, as a mere will-o'-the-wisp. The belief in it which later on took hold of Mediæval Europe had not yet met with any general sort of acceptance, though the Arabian school in the main adopted it, and there seems little doubt that it was held by Michael Scot himself. One book indeed on this particular subject, *De Alchimia*, is attributed to his pen. The book is contained in a manuscript in possession of Corpus Christi College, Oxford. If, however, the main part of the work is genuine, which is somewhat uncertain, the dedication to Theophilus, King of the Scots, is certainly not so. We have in this book a curious formula for turning lead into gold, which runs as follows :

Medibibaz, the Saracen of Africa, used it to change lead into gold in the following manner:—Take lead and melt it thrice with caustic (comburenti), red arsenic, sublimate of vitriol, sugar of alum, and with that red tuchia of India which is found on the shore of the Red Sea, and let the whole be again and again quenched in the juice of the Portulaca marina, the wild cucumber, a solution of sal ammoniac, and the urine of a young badger. Let all these ingredients then, when well mixed, be set on the fire, with the addition of some common salt, and well boiled until they be reduced to one-third of their original bulk, when you must proceed to distil them with care. Then take the marchasite of gold, prepared talc, roots of coral, some carcharoot, which is an herb very like the Portulaca marina; alum of Cumæ, something red and saltish, Roman alum and vitriol, and let the latter be made red; sugar of alum, Cyprus earth, some of the red Barbary earth, for that gives a good colour; Cumæan earth of the red sort, African tuchia, which is a stone of variegated colours and being melted with copper changeth it into gold; Cumæan salt which is pure red arsenic, the blood of a ruddy man, red tartar, gumma of Barbary, which is red and worketh wonders in this art; salt of Sardinia which is like. . . . Let all these be beaten together in a brazen mortar, then sifted finely and made into a paste with the above water. Dry this paste, and again rub it fine on the marble slab. Then take the lead you have prepared as directed above, and melt it together with the powder, adding some red alum, and some more of the various salts. This alum is found about Aleppo (Alapia), and in Armenia, and will give your metal a good colour. When you have so done you shall see the lead changed into the finest gold, as good as what comes from Arabia. This have I, Michael Scot, often put to the proof and ever found it to be true.

Whether the statement appearing in the manuscript under his name, that Michael Scot worked on this recipe, be true or not, one would not envy the task of the modern chemist who was called upon to compound the prescription. The basic idea of alchemy which, since the discovery of radium, is looked upon with some favour by certain advanced scientists, that all metals are reducible to a single substance, and therefore theoretically interchangeable, does not seem to find much place in this curious prescription, which suggests the idea of what we should call to-day a gold-substitute, rather than the genuine metal itself, in spite of the fact that we are told that the gold in question would prove " as good as what comes from Arabia."

The greatest work of Scot as translator was his reproduction in Latin of the commentary of Averroes on the *De Anima* of Aristotle. This book, which expounded views on theological problems which were the reverse of orthodox, was long held back from publication by Scot's patron, the Emperor Frederick, who hesitated to incur obloquy, and in especial the hostility of the Pope by reason of its publication. Friction, however, between the Papal See and the Emperor became so acute in the end that it appeared useless to attempt to placate papal bigotry further, and the publication in question was thus finally given to the world.

The study of the writings of Averroes had indeed taken very strong hold on Scot's imagination, and if the story may be accepted as authentic, he even went so far as to attempt to evoke the spirit of the great Arabian, presumably with a view to securing his assistance in the work which he had in hand. There is nothing intrinsically improbable in the supposition that Scott practised or experimented in such methods of evocation. Averroes had only been dead some twenty years when Scot was in Spain, and holding the views he did, he may well have thought that the philosopher's spirit had not passed so far from the physical plane that some form of necromantic conjuration of his conscious personality would be ineffectual. Here, as elsewhere, it seems impossible to draw the line between record of fact and that fabric of legend and tradition which has been woven round the story of his life.

A number of the tales told of Scot's magical achievements reduce themselves in the light of modern knowledge to the results of highly developed hypnotic powers. It is familiar knowledge that such achievements are not unknown in India at the present day. A Florentine authority gives us one of these anecdotes. Scot's guests at dinner, we are told, once asked him to show them a new marvel. The month was January. Yet in spite of the season he caused vines with fresh shoots and ripe grapes to appear on the table. The company were bidden each of them to choose a bunch, but their host warned them not to put forth their hands till he should give the sign. At the word "Cut!" lo, the grapes disappeared, and the guests found themselves each with a knife in the one hand and in the other his neighbour's sleeve. Another story of a more or less similar character is told of a feast given by the Emperor to celebrate his coronation at Rome, which took place on November 22, 1220.

The pages were still on foot with ewers and basins of perfumed water and embroidered towels, when suddenly Michael Scot appeared with a companion, both of them dressed in Eastern robes, and offered to show the guests a marvel. The weather was oppressively warm, so Frederick asked him to procure them a shower of rain which might bring coolness. This the magician did accordingly, raising a great storm, which as suddenly vanished again at their pleasure. Being required by the Emperor to name his reward, Scot asked leave to choose one of the company to be the champion of himself and his friend against certain enemies of theirs. This being freely granted, their choice fell on Ulfo, a German baron. As it seemed to Ulfo, they set off at once on their expedition, leaving the coasts of Sicily in two great galleys, and with a mighty following of armed men. They sailed through the Gulf of Lyons, and passed by the Pillars of Hercules, into the unknown and western sea. Here they found smiling coasts, received a welcome from the strange people, and joined themselves to the army of the place; Ulfo taking the supreme command. Two pitched battles and a successful siege formed the incidents of the campaign. Ulfo killed the hostile king, married his lovely daughter, and reigned in his stead; Michael and his companion having left to seek other adventures. Of this marriage sons and daughters were begotten, and twenty years passed like a dream ere the magicians returned, and invited their champion to revisit the Sicilian court. Ulfo went back with them, but what was his amazement, on entering the palace of Palermo, to find everything just as it had been at the moment of their departure so long before; even the pages were still holding rounds with water for the hands of the Emperor's guests. This prodigy performed, Michael and the other withdrew and were seen no more; but Ulfo, it is said, remained ever inconsolable for the lost land of loveliness, and the joys of wedded life he had left behind for ever, in a dream not to be repeated.

On Scot's return to the court of Frederick II., after his sojourn in Sicily, he added the study and practice of the medical art to his other activities. Lesley states that he "gained much praise as a philosopher, astronomer, and physician," and Dempster speaks of him as "one of the first physicians for learning." He appears to have treated cases which would not yield to the ordinary medical pharmacopœia, and in particular he specialised in leprosy, gout, and dropsy. Acting apparently under his advice, Frederick II. instituted various reforms in the practice of medicine. It was stipulated that the course preliminary to qualification should consist of three years in arts, and five in medicine and surgery. Laws were passed forbidding the adulteration of drugs, while physicians were prohibited from demanding a greater fee than half a *taren* of gold per day, and this gave the patient the right to be visited three times in the course of the twenty-four hours. It was stipulated that the poor should be attended free of charge. Certain recipes of Michael Scot's are still extant, and can be studied in Latin in the British Museum. One of these bears the name of the *Pillulæ Magistri Michaelis Scoti*. They seem to be something in the nature of a universal panacea, and perhaps if the prescription were taken up by some enterprising modern chemist, they might rival the fame of the celebrated Beecham's Pills!

It appears that Scot had ambitions in the way of ecclesiastical preferment; but though the Emperor put himself out to secure his favourite the position which he coveted, and in fact appealed to the Pope on his behalf, nothing practical came of these representations. Probably Scot's fame was of too dubious a kind to recommend him to the heads of the orthodox Church, and the Archbishop of Canterbury, to whom the Pope applied in his interest, does not seem to have responded in any friendly fashion. Finally, an offer was made to Michael Scot of the Archbishopric of Cashel in Ireland, but in those days the Irish were little better than a barbarous race, and they spoke the language of Erse, which was a sealed book to their prospective bishop. In any case, though the Chapter had actually elected him to the post, he decided to decline. He apparently had too much principle to accept the position of an absentee bishop, and a home among a wild and uncultured race would hardly have been to the liking of a man who had associated with the most intellectual minds of Europe. These hopes of ecclesiastical preferment having fallen through, Frederick, after long delay, decided to take steps for the publication of the translation of the works of Averroes, and certain books of Aristotle, with the commentaries thereon of the Arabian philosophers. He issued an imperial circular announcing the appearance of these, and sent Michael Scot as his emissary to arrange for their publication in the principal European centres of learning. Finally, after visiting Bologna and Paris, Scot made his way to England, where he appears to have visited Oxford about the year 1230. Tradition says that he journeyed thence to his native land of Scotland. But shortly after this we lose sight of him altogether, and though there is no authoritative evidence with regard to his death, he seems to have passed away by or before the year 1232. In this year the *Abbreviatio Avicennæ* was published at Melfi, in the Latin version which Scot had translated. Henry of Colonia was selected by Frederick to transcribe the work from the imperial copy, and Scot's biographer is probably right in regarding this work as a wreath laid by his imperial friend on his grave.

MICHAEL SCOT 73

The matter would assuredly have been placed in Scot's own hands if he were still alive.

Scot is related to have foretold that his death would take place by the blow of a stone falling on his head, and tradition says that being in church one day with head uncovered at the sacring of the mass, a stone, shaken from the tower by the motion of the bell rope, fell upon his head, mortally wounding him. Presumably this incident occurred in Scotland; if, that is, there is any truth at all in the story.

Another prediction is also attributed to Michael Scot by the same chronicler—Pipini. He states that he foretold the manner also of the Emperor's death, which he declared would take place "ad portas ferreas"; that is, "at the iron gates," and in a town named after Flora. Frederick, it is said, interpreted this as referring to Florence, which city he accordingly made a point of avoiding. During his last campaign, however, in the year 1250, he fell ill at Florentino, in Apulia, where he slept in a chamber of the castle. His bed, says the story, stood against a wall recently built to fill up the ancient gateway of the tower, the iron staples on which the gate had been hung still forming part of the wall. It is stated that the Emperor, learning these particulars, and calling to mind Michael Scot's prediction, exclaimed, "This is the place where I shall make an end, as it was told me. The will of God be done, for here I shall die." A few days later the great Emperor passed to his rest.

Of Michael Scot's learning and erudition there can be no question, in spite of the unfavourable criticisms of Roger Bacon with regard to his knowledge of languages, which are the less worthy of notice in view of the fact that Bacon's own accomplishments in this direction were far inferior to those of Scot. A fairer criticism of his work would be based on its lack of originality, and the fact that the greater part of his literary output was borrowed either from the Arabians or the Greeks. His talents as a past master of mathematics were never in dispute, and his researches into the problems presented by astronomy enjoyed a great vogue in his own day.

While there is no evidence but that of highly-coloured tradition to suggest that Michael Scot was the adept he is represented as being in magical spells and incantations, there is nothing in our historical knowledge of his career which renders the practice of such arts by him at all incredible, or indeed unlikely. Legend has magnified this portion of his many-sided activities to the exclusion of that branch of his labours which might well, one would have thought, have earned for him more enduring fame. The lovers of the marvellous have thus surrounded with a mysterious and semi-sinister halo the name of a man whose chief work in life lay in the paths of philosophy, astronomy, and medical research. It seems not improbable that the last of these pursuits led this daring thinker into the investigation and practice of what to-day we term hypnotism, and its employment to the bewilderment of his acquaintances in the creation of illusions, the source of which we now recognise in the power of a master mind to mould by sheer force of will the plastic imagination and subjective consciousness of his audience.

IV

PARACELSUS

THE embattled forces of conservative orthodoxy are so strong that one is sometimes tempted to wonder how it is that the world ever goes round at all; how it is that the forward movement of progress succeeds, as it apparently does, in getting the better of so many retrograde tendencies, so much prejudice, so strong a clinging to the stereotyped conditions of the day. After all, the more one thinks about it, the more one becomes convinced that the whole progress of the world is the work of the very, very few; that the positive and progressive intellect is the rare exception, and that if democratic conditions really prevailed (as of course they never do) all civilisation would go backwards and gradually revert once more to chaos. What a mockery, after all, Democracy is! And how hopelessly the modern world is deluded in thinking that anywhere or at any time Democracy has in reality held sway! As a matter of fact, the many have never ruled, have never wished to rule;

PARACELSUS

they have merely asked for some strong man to lead them. Where was ever the flock of sheep that did not follow the bell-wether? Here and there we meet with a master mind that—for good or evil—leads the multitude—or, if he does not lead, at least points the way where others will eventually follow. Side by side with him we see the multitude either drifting or being led. "Work!" said Voltaire, that most popular of writers, "work for the little public!" Voltaire knew, as all great leaders have known, before and after, that it is the "little public" that ever dominates the situation. It is the "little leaven that leaveneth the whole lump." "It is a sight beloved of the gods," says the old saying, "to see a good man struggling against adversity." But is it not a finer sight still, to see a strong man battling with the forces of orthodoxy, and refusing to yield his ground? A man of such a mould was Philip Bombast of Hohenheim, better known by his assumed name of Paracelsus. Never was there any one to whom Shelley's celebrated line

> The sun comes out and many reptiles spawn,

was more absolutely appropriate. The hostility and venomous antagonism of his own profession, with a few notable exceptions, followed and persecuted him throughout his entire medical career.

The boldness and independence of his medical attitude galled the leaders as well as the rank and file of the profession. But what was still more galling to them than his lack of orthodoxy, was the fact that his novel methods, as they must have appeared to the doctors of that day, were so immeasurably more successful than their own. Paracelsus, indeed, never gave nor asked for quarter. John the Baptist denouncing the Pharisees who came to him as "a generation of vipers" was no bad parallel to Paracelsus's stinging invective on the ignorance and tradition-loving proclivities of his own profession.

Many to whom the name of Paracelsus is familiar are accustomed to look upon him as little more than a singularly successful quack who revived the traditions of an earlier school of Occultism in defiance of the more scientific methods of his own time. As a matter of fact, the doctors of his day were, in the vast majority of cases, merely theorists with little real practical experience, but with a fair store of book-learning of a very indifferent kind. It was Paracelsus whose medical knowledge was derived from experiment and experience, and who had acquired the greater part of his medical and surgical skill from wide and varied travelling and visiting more countries and more different nationalities than any other medical expert of his day, and who had learnt by actual association with all

PARACELSUS (aged 24)
From a painting by Scorel (1517), now in the Louvre Gallery.

sorts and conditions of men in different climes, far more than any book-learning had ever taught him. The period of Paracelsus's career coincided with the Reformation of Luther, and with the wider and more general Renaissance movement. This latter development had brought back in its train the study of classical learning and classical ideals which had fallen into discredit about the period of the first triumph of Christianity and its establishment as a world-religion. The attitude of the earlier Christians, who looked upon the Pagan deities as devils, and Greek and Roman classical writers as apologists for devil-worship, had passed away; and the highest dignitaries of the Church were now often noted for their classical erudition and ripe scholarship. With the return of classical ideals came back also into favour in a number of unexpected quarters the doctrines of Neoplatonism. When Hypatia perished at Alexandria, orthodox Christianity set its foot on Plotinus and all his works. The struggle at the end had been one rather between Christianity and the later Greek philosophers with their Neoplatonic conceptions than between Christianity and Pagan Rome. The gods of Rome were dead already. Pan was dead past resurrecting. The danger that threatened Christianity was the triumph of such Emperors as Julian the Apostate— Julian, whose master was Plotinus, and whose religion was Neoplatonism merely dressed in an old Roman garb. To the thinkers and philosophers of that time the triumph of Christianity seemed like the victory of exoteric religion over the inner esoteric truths. Back, now, with all that was best of the scholarship and art of Greece and Rome, came the mystic doctrines of the Alexandrian philosophers—back, not in triumph, but daring once more to reassert themselves in the face of a hostile world that had long even forgotten their existence. A thousand years separated Hypatia from Cornelius Agrippa—a thousand years which, in the realm of thought, might well be characterised as the Dark Ages. Cornelius Agrippa von Nettesheim was born at Cologne in 1486. Seven years later, on 10th November 1493, at Einsiedeln, near Zurich, a son was born to Dr Wilhelm Bombast von Hohenheim, and was christened Theophrastus, in honour of Theophrastus Tyrtamos, a Greek physician, philosopher, and follower of Aristotle. This child was subsequently to be known to fame and held up to obloquy under the title of Paracelsus.

It was a period in which the world was in labour with great events. Only a year before Columbus had landed on American soil. In the same year, or the previous one, passed away a man whose life was destined to create as great a revolution in the

PARACELSUS

history of the human race as that of Columbus himself—William Caxton. Returning from a long sojourn in the Netherlands in or about 1474, Caxton established his printing press in the precincts of Westminster Abbey, and before his death at least sixty-four books are known to have been issued from this first English Printing House. Ten years exactly before Paracelsus's birth, a third of these great makers of revolutions had seen the light. On 10th November 1483, Martin Luther was born at Eisleben in Lower Saxony, and when the subject of these notes was twenty-four years old, Luther nailed his ninety-five theses against the Doctrine of Indulgences on the church door at Wittemberg. Paracelsus, when occasion offered, did not attempt to disguise his sympathy with this bold reformer, though he took no actual part in the movement, and he was accused by his enemies of being a medical Luther, a charge which he took pains to show that he did not in any way resent. Another noteworthy character in the realm of History and Literature, Lorenzo de Medici, had passed away a year before our hero's birth. In England the Wars of the Roses were over, and Henry VII. was busy establishing monarchy on a firm basis, the people, worn out by incessant struggles, being glad to accept the Tudor rule, sympathetic as it always was to the middle and commercial classes. In

Europe there was no Austrian Emperor, and Italy was still fated, for centuries to come, to remain a geographical expression. The Holy Roman Empire extended from the German Ocean and the Baltic Sea on the North to the Adriatic on the South. Poland and Lithuania extended far along its Eastern border, and the outmost limit of the realm of the Muscovite was still 500 miles east of the site where a century later Peter the Great was to found and give his name to the capital of the Russian Empire. The conquering Turk was thundering at the gates of Christendom. Ferdinand and Isabella, patrons of Columbus, reigned at Madrid. Everywhere throughout the civilised world vast changes were impending, everywhere the horizon was widening, and men's minds were being directed into new channels and to fresh fields of enterprise and of opinion.

There has been much discussion as to what exactly is connoted by the name "Paracelsus," and how it came to be first adopted. What seems clear is that von Hohenheim adopted the name himself, and was not, as some have held, given it by his admirers. It was a usual practice in those days to write books under some Latin *nom de plume*, frequently some adaptation into Latin of the name of the writer. In all probability the last two syllables of the name, "celsus," were suggested by

"Hohen" (or "high"), "Hohenheim" being literally translated as "high home." With regard to the first two syllables it is noticeable that these were occasionally employed by Paracelsus in giving name to his medical treatises. There is thus one treatise called "Paramirum," and another "Paragranum." This word "para" seems to have been used in the sense of giving the word to which it was prefixed a superlative value. Thus "Paramirum" would mean "extremely wonderful." The whole word is doubtless a polyglot hotchpotch, the first part being Greek and the second Latin; but mediæval writers had little scruple in adapting the classical tongues to their own requirements.

To follow the writings of Paracelsus it is necessary to understand his phraseology, his jargon, as we should call it in the slang of to-day. Without this he is as incomprehensible as is the dog Latin of a scientific textbook to one who is not a scientific specialist—or, to give another example, as the language of Astrology is to one who is not an Astrologer. Paracelsus held that there were three basic substances necessary to the existence of all bodies. These he called Sulphur, Mercury, and Salt. Sulphur corresponds to fire, or rather to the principle of inflammability; Mercury to water, or fluidity; and Salt to earth, or solidity. For a full glossary of the terms which he employed, readers are referred to the volume on *The Life and Philosophy of Paracelsus*, by the late Dr Franz Hartmann. In this terminology *Azoth* stands for the creative principle in Nature, or the spiritual vitalising force; the *Ilech Primum* is the causative force; *Cherio*, the essence of the thing, the "fifth principle," which constitutes what we call its essential qualities; the *Evestrum* is man's astral body, his ethereal counterpart, that may act to him as guardian angel and warn him of dangers; the *Elementaries* are the astral corpses of the dead, and must not be confused with the *Elementals*, or Nature Spirits —Sylphs, Salamanders, Undines, and Gnomes; *Magic* is the conscious employment of spiritual powers to act on external Nature. Many of these expressions have been adopted by the Theosophists of the present day and by students of Occultism.

It is clear, though Paracelsus long antedated Hahnemann, the founder of Homœopathy, that much of his medical teaching is what we should now call Homœopathic. Hahnemann, in fact, borrowed extensively from Paracelsus. Take, for instance, Paracelsus's teaching with regard to the quintessence or virtue of each substance. This, he taught, though infinitesimal in quantity, even in large bodies, had none the less the power to affect the mass through and through, as a single drop of gall embitters, or a few grains of saffron colour a large quantity of water. The application of homœopathic cures by those ignorant of homœopathic principles has frequently led to mistakes in this connection ; as, for instance, the administration of doses many times in excess of what the complaint requires, the result being the entire failure of the medicine to produce the intended effect.

" There are wide differences," says Paracelsus, striking again a very homœopathic note, "between what the ancient doctors taught and what we here teach, and therefore our healing art differs widely from theirs. For we teach that what heals a man also wounds him, and what wounded will also heal him. For the nettle can be so changed that it cannot burn, the flame so that it does not scorch, and the chelidony so that it does not cicatrize. Thus similars are good in healing, such and such a salt to such and such a sore. And the things which heal a wound in Nature heal the same sort of wound in man."

"Many kinds of rust," says Paracelsus again, "occur in the minerals ; for each mineral has its own peculiar nature." This rust is in the form of a disease, and iron has one disease, while copper has another. In a similar way a man has a sore and it is healed by treatment. The metal, too, has a sore, and can be healed by treatment. "Metallic bodies," says Paracelsus, long antedating the discoveries of the present day, "are as liable to death as the others, for their salt is arsenic." The whole earth is linked together, and the life that passes through the bodies of men passes also through the bodies of minerals. Paracelsus had no patience with those who taught of a panacea that would heal all diseases. He described them as people who "rode all horses with one saddle," through whom more harm than good was effected. He maintained that a doctor must know the sick and all matters appertaining to their state "just as a carpenter knows his wood." He mentions six essential qualifications for the practical physician.

(1) A doctor (he says) must know how many kinds of tissue there are in the body, and how each kind stands in relation to the man.

(2) He must know all the bones, such as the ribs and their coverings, the difference between one and another, their relations to each other and their articulations.

(3) He must know all the blood-vessels, the nerves, the cartilages and how they are held together.

(4) He must know the length, number, form, condition, and purpose of each member of the body, its particular flesh, marrow, and all other details.

(5) He must know where all emunctoria lie and how they are to be averted ; also what is in every cavity of the body, and everything about the intestines.

(6) He must with all his might and being seek to understand about life and death, what the chief organs in man mean, and what each member can and may suffer.

If we look to Paracelsus as the real founder of Homœopathy, so also must we regard him as the pioneer of magnetism and magnetic healing. Man, he maintained, is nourished through the magnetic power which resides in all Nature and by which each individual being draws its specific nourishment to itself. He called this magnetic force *Mumia* in his special phraseology, and he laid great stress on the healing power which resided in this *Mumia*. " Just as the power of the lily breaks forth in perfume which is invisible, so," he writes, " the invisible body sends forth its healing influence. Just as in the visible body are wonderful activities which the senses can perceive, so, too, lie powers in the invisible body which can work great wonders." To him the whole universe was one, and knit together by indissoluble bonds.

" The astral currents created by the imagination of the Macrocosmos," he writes, " act upon the Microcosmos, and produce certain states in the latter, and likewise the astral currents produced by the imagination and will of man produce certain states in external Nature ; and these currents may reach far, because the power of the imagination reaches as far as thought can go. The physiological processes taking place in the body of living beings are caused by their astral currents, and the physiological and meteorological processes taking place in the great organism of Nature are caused by the astral currents of Nature as a whole. The astral currents of either act upon the other, either consciously or unconsciously ; and if this fact is properly understood it will cease to appear incredible that the mind of man may produce changes in the universal mind, which may cause changes in the atmosphere—winds and rains, storm, hail and lightning—or that evil may be changed into good by the power of Faith. Heaven is a field into which the imagination of man throws the seeds."

Here, in a single paragraph, is the philosophy of Astrology, and the justification for the efficacy of prayer.

I have said that Paracelsus was the father of Homœopathy, and the father also of that later school of animal magnetism which was founded in France in the latter part of the eighteenth century, and the inception of which is always associated with the name of Mesmer. Unfortunately, Mesmer had neither the knowledge nor the experience, nor yet the intuitive faculties of his master, Paracelsus. But, resurrected as it was under somewhat unfavourable conditions, there is reason to believe that magnetic healing is destined to play a far greater part in the future of medical art than it has ever done in the past. Not only was Paracelsus a pioneer in Homœopathy and animal magnetism, he was also one of the first, as well as one of the greatest, of all Faith-healers. "Faith," he says, "has a great deal more power than the physical body." "All magical processes are based upon Faith." "The power of Faith overcomes all spirits of Nature, because it is a spiritual power, and Spirit is higher than Nature." "Whatever is grown in the realm of Nature may be changed by the power of Faith." "Anything we may accomplish which surpasses Nature is accomplished by Faith, and by Faith diseases may be cured." "Imagination," he says again, "is the cause of many diseases. Faith is the cure for all." "If we cannot cure a disease by Faith, it is because our Faith is too weak. But our Faith is weak on account of our want of knowledge. If we were conscious of the power of God within ourselves, we should never fail." "The power of amulets does not rest so much in the material of which they are made as in the Faith with which they are worn." Paracelsus's chosen motto was:

Alterius non sit qui suus esse potest—

"Let him not belong to another who has the power to be his own"—who can, in short, be master of his own soul. Paracelsus declined to follow any leader, but formed his own conclusions from his own experience. For him the *Codex Naturæ* was a system which led straight to exact knowledge, and he rejected whatever could not be verified by research. He laid the foundations of a new system, built on evidence rather than on the outworn traditions of the medicine of his day. This system comprised within itself at once a practical guide to the medical art and a spiritual philosophy of life. The fatal error of divorcing the physical from the spiritual, and treating the physical as a thing apart, which has rendered abortive so much of the medical research of recent generations, would undoubtedly have been obviated, had the modern exponent of the medical art realised that in Paracelsus was to be found a pioneer who brought the life-giving genius of his intellect to bear on old truths in their relation to modern problems, rather than a quack and mountebank who deluded his contemporaries—none so easy a task—into the idea that he had accomplished marvellous cures where the medical faculty of his day could show nothing but a record of failures.

V

EMANUEL SWEDENBORG

OF all the men and women whom the world has classed under the general title of " mystic," not one certainly occupies so singular a position as Emanuel Swedenborg. If we decide to accept the world's verdict—and it seems difficult to do otherwise—and agree to call Swedenborg a mystic, we are confronted by the fact that we can find no parallel either to his personality or to his career, though we search the roll of the mystics of all the ages. Pascal indeed was, like Swedenborg, a master mathematician, and a man of wide general learning, but he was a mystic first and foremost, and his life from an early date was given up to his calling as a leading light of the Catholic Church. Swedenborg, on the other hand, was, until the age of fifty, a man of science and a man of affairs ; that is, he was a scientist of the most eminently practical kind, one whose encyclopædic knowledge was turned always into utilitarian channels, and for whom knowledge of any kind appeared to have no meaning outside its practical application. It would be difficult to instance a single one of the world's great men whose interests were so wide, or whose mental activity was so all-absorbing. Outside art there seemed literally nothing that did not appeal to him as a field for his indefatigable investigation, and, as regards art, it was presumably its lack of utilitarian value which led to its neglect by his essentially practical mentality.

Swedenborg started his travels in the first years of early manhood, and wherever they took him there was nothing which escaped his observant eye. To whatever part of Europe he went it would seem that he could not be satisfied without learning all that was to be learnt, without seeing all that was to be seen. When he establishes himself in London he does not merely take lodgings because the price is reasonable or because the cooking is good, or because he thinks he will be comfortable. He writes from London in 1711 : " I turn my lodgings to some use, and change them often. At first I was at a watchmaker's, and now I am at a mathematical instrument maker's. From them I steal their trades, which some day will be of use to me." At Leyden he learnt to grind glass for lenses, so that he might furnish himself with appliances which he could not afford to buy. His brother wishes for globes for the university at Upsala. These proved too expensive, and he was asked to purchase printed

To face p. 92

EMANUEL SWEDENBORG

maps which might be mounted in Sweden. The makers would not supply these, so Swedenborg applied himself to learning engraving, and prepared them himself. When chafing at enforced inactivity at home he turns his attention to music, and writes to his brother-in-law that he has been able several times to take the place of the organist. In travelling on the Continent he studies the fortifications of the towns, the methods of constructing fences. He visits and investigates all the manufactories. He passes critical remarks with regard to the blast furnaces, the vitriol, arsenic, and sulphur works, the copper and tin manufactories, the paper mills, and studies also the methods of mining. Not content with this, he investigates the social conditions of the people, criticises the situation of affairs in France, the wealth of the Church and the poverty of the people. "Everywhere," he says, "the convents, churches, and monks are the wealthiest and possess most land. The monks are fat, puffed up, and prosperous. A whole proud army might be formed of them without their being missed." Again: "The houses are miserable, the convents magnificent, the people poor and wretched." He investigates the problem of the revenue of the French Government, obtained by the system of taxation called tithing. "It amounts," he says, "to some thirty-two million livres, and Paris, on account of its rents, contributes nearly two-thirds of the sum." "I am told," he says, "that the ecclesiastical order possesses one-fifth of all the property in the State, and that the country will be ruined if this goes on much longer."[1] He gives the number of convents in France, actually at that date between fourteen and fifteen thousand; the number of the members of the religious orders; the number of the abbesses, prioresses, chapters, etc. He goes to hear the celebrated preachers, among them the King's chaplain, who "gesticulates like an actor." He discusses the adoration of saints with an abbé. He visits the hospitals and attends the opening of Parliament. Not content with this, he frequents the opera and the theatres, and passes opinions upon the most popular pieces and the most distinguished actors and actresses. In the midst of all this we find him speculating on the form of the particles of the atmosphere, and writing an introductory essay to a book which he is planning to prove that " the soul of wisdom is the knowledge and acknowledgment of the Supreme Being." As if this were not enough, he occupies his spare moments in the study of anatomy, astronomy, magnetism, and hydrostatics.

Surely, since the world began, there was never a more versatile brain! He has even observations to

[1] Church property being free from taxation.

make on military matters. He goes to see the Brandenburg soldiers, Frederick the Great's famous regiment. "The men," he says, "are tall and slender and they march erectly. They go through their drills with the greatest promptness and regularity, but their manner is a little theatrical. The whole squadron is like a machine placed there, moving instantaneously at the pleasure of the machinist." "If," he says, "they displayed the same uniformity in battle as in drill, they would conquer Alexander's army, and subject a great part of Europe to Prussia, but——" He leaves it to the reader to fill in the reason of his doubt.

Others besides Swedenborg have possessed that encyclopædic type of brain which amasses vast stores of miscellaneous knowledge, but few, if any, have possessed at the same time Swedenborg's extraordinary capacity for utilising the knowledge gained and turning it to practical account. The idea of learning as an object in itself was indeed entirely alien to Swedenborg's type of mentality. All information acquired was merely regarded as a means towards some practical end. We thus find him founding universal principles upon the knowledge he has accumulated in explanation of the laws which govern phenomena. We see him, for example, deducing his conclusions in the field of geology from a number of observed facts. He reports on the geological conformation of Sweden, and concludes from it that the country was at one time swept over by a sea in a state of great commotion. He notices the fact that the stones on the mountain sides are worn off and rounded, in support of this. He also describes the remnants of a wrecked ship excavated far inland, and the skeleton of a whale which was discovered in West Gothland. " Swedenborg's contributions in the field of geology," says Professor A. G. Nathorst, " are of such significance and value that they alone would have been sufficient to have secured him an honoured scientific name." As a mining expert he was unequalled. " We should never be able to finish," says Professor Schleiden, " if we attempted to enumerate all the improvements which Swedenborg introduced in the working of the mines in his own country." "The metallurgical works of this remarkable man," says Dr Percy, " seem to be very imperfectly known, and yet none are in my judgment more worthy of the attention of those interested in the history of metallurgy." The air-tight stove which he describes in his work on *New Observations and Discoveries Respecting Iron and Fire*, published in 1721, is stated to be identical in principle with one recently patented in Washington.[1] Sir Isaac

[1] See *Life of Emanuel Swedenborg*. By George Trobridge. London : Frederick Warne & Co. To which book I must acknowledge my great indebtedness.

EMANUEL SWEDENBORG

Newton had propounded the corpuscular theory of light, which was for long universally held. Swedenborg dissented, stating, in his *Principia*, that "motion diffused from a given centre through a contiguous medium or volume of particles of ether produced light." This theory is the one now adopted. Swedenborg also notices that light and electricity are produced by the same efficient cause, thereby supplying the clue to the utilisation of electricity as a means of lighting. Even where in the field of science he was looked upon as a dreamer in his own days, his dreams have since taken practical shape. Among the inventions which he projected was " the plan of a certain ship which with its men was to go under the surface of the sea wherever it chooses, and do great damage to the fleet of the enemy." He also designed a flying machine, a project which he was very reluctant to drop. Christopher Polhem, however, threw cold water on this, saying, with respect to flying by artificial means, " there is perhaps the same difficulty as in making a *perpetuum mobile*, or gold by artificial means."

His philosophy recognises the synthetical as well as the analytical method as requisite to arrive at true conclusions. " Both," he says, " are necessary in reflecting upon and tracing out one and the same thing ; for in order to do so there is required both light, *a priori*, and experience, *a posteriori*." " He who is possessed of scientific knowledge," he says elsewhere, " and is merely skilled in experiment, had taken only the first steps in wisdom. For such a person is only acquainted with what is posterior, and is ignorant of what is prior. Thus his wisdom does not extend beyond the working of the senses and is unconnected with reason ; whereas, nevertheless, true wisdom embraces both."

Unquestionably Swedenborg, as he is known to us from the record of the first fifty years of his life (if we except the earliest years of his childhood), was about the last person one would expect to have his name associated with that Swedenborgian gospel by which eventually it came to be known to the world at large. He had, as we have seen, earned many titles to recognition, but assuredly that of a medium of communication between this world and the world of spirits was not one of them.

Swedenborg's father was a Swedish Lutheran Bishop with leanings towards pietism, and a rather broader and more sympathetic outlook than the majority of his fellow clergy. His name, Swedborg, was subsequently changed to Swedenborg when the family was ennobled by the Swedish king. Emanuel was the second son and third child of Bishop Swedborg and his wife, Anna, of whom we know but little,

EMANUEL SWEDENBORG

and who died when Emanuel was only eight years old. The child was thus surrounded by religious influences in his early days, and it is said that his father had a guardian angel with whom he claimed to be able to hold converse on occasion. Reared under these conditions, he naturally enough evinced strongly religious tendencies in his childhood. "From my fourth to my tenth year," he says, "I was constantly engaged in thought upon God, salvation, and the spiritual experiences of men. I revealed things at which my father and mother wondered, saying that angels must be speaking through me." Here at least we obtain some suggestion of what he eventually became, and of which the intervening years between childhood and middle age seem to afford us little or no hint. The believer in heredity will point to the psychic temperament of the father as inherited by the son; but there appears to be no foreshadowing in his ancestry of that encyclopædic mind with which he was destined to astonish his contemporaries. His father evidently failed to understand his precocious son, and the relations between the two were far from cordial, the son considering that his father was inappreciative and failed to encourage his intellectual activities, and also blaming him for meanness in matters of finance. Bishop Swedborg had, however, eight other children besides Emanuel, and very probably he did not find it easy to make two ends meet, especially as he was something of an author himself, and published books at his own expense, which proved far from remunerative. Probably the father considered that the son ought to settle down to some regular trade or profession instead of commencing life by travelling in search of knowledge first to one country and then to another. Presumably he regarded his precocious offspring as likely to become a jack-of-all-trades and master of none, and there are doubtless many other parents who, under similar circumstances, would have thought the same. In any case the son was able to start off on his travels in spite of financial embarrassments and many dangers on the way. He was nearly wrecked when approaching England. Then the ship was boarded by pirates, and on the top of this was fired into by a British guardship, being mistaken for the pirate craft. Finally, our youthful hero narrowly escaped hanging for breaking the quarantine regulations, the plague at this time being prevalent in Sweden. Under somewhat similar circumstances the great Julius told the captain of his vessel not to be afraid, as he was carrying Cæsar. Whether Swedenborg had any such faith in a Providence watching over his future destiny, we are not told. He certainly realised his unique powers, but can hardly have suspected the channel into which they were eventually to be diverted. The one link between Emanuel and his family was his brother-in-law, Eric Benzelius, afterwards bishop, and the sister to whom he was married. In his financial and other troubles he repeatedly appeals to him for sympathy and practical help, evidently not without response. He also asks for intercession with his father, to whom he obviously did not care to appeal direct, having met with too many rebuffs. It is interesting to note that one of the first objects that met his eyes in London was " the magnificent St Paul's Cathedral, finished a few days ago, in all its parts." He makes the acquaintance of Flamsteed, the most notable astronomer in England, who was concerned in the founding of Greenwich Observatory and seems to have been something of an astrologer as well. Apparently as the result of this visit, he takes up with enthusiasm the study of astronomy.

I have made such progress in it [he says], as to have discovered much which I think will be useful in its study. Although in the beginning it made my brain ache, yet long speculations are no longer difficult for me. I examined closely all proportions for finding the terrestrial longitude, but could not find a single one. I have, therefore, originated a method by means of the Moon, which is unerring, and I am certain that it is the best which has yet been advanced. In a short time I will inform the

Royal Society that I have a proposition to make on this subject, stating my points. . . . I have also discovered many new methods for observing the planets, the Moon, and the stars. That which concerns the Moon and its parallax, diameter, and inequality I will publish whenever an opportunity arises.

He longs to go to Oxford, and investigate the Bodleian Library, but cannot, for want of money. "I wonder," he says, "my father does not show greater care for me than to let me live now for more than sixteen months upon 250 rixdalers (something under £50)." Finally, he returns home and obtains an appointment as Assessor-extraordinary at the State Department of the Board of Mines, which was responsible for the supervision of the great mining industries of Sweden. In this connection he is fortunate in making the acquaintance of Christopher Polhem, the celebrated engineer, who recommends him for his talents and readiness of resource. By degrees he becomes an intimate guest with Polhem's family, a circumstance which leads in the end to a tragic love affair. He falls desperately in love with Polhem's younger daughter. The father gives his consent; but the girl, a mere child of thirteen or fourteen, cannot reconcile herself to the idea. Swedenborg, with great sorrow, relinquishes his claim, resolving never again to let his thoughts settle upon any woman. Polhem himself seems to have been almost equally distressed with Swedenborg over the incident, especially as it led to a breach between himself and the young man, whom he had come to regard in the light of his own son. A period of depression follows, which is accentuated by the death of Charles XII. of Sweden, about the same period, from whose encouragement and support Emanuel had considerable expectations. The relations between himself and the King were, indeed, singularly intimate, Charles readily appreciating the young man's remarkable talents and mathematical knowledge. " Every day," says Swedenborg, in writing on 14th September 1718, " I had some mathematical matters for his Majesty, who deigned to be pleased with all of them. When the eclipse took place, I took his Majesty out to see it, and talked much to him about it. This, however, is a mere beginning."

In the summer of 1721, Swedenborg started again on his travels, his object this time being to study the mines and manufactories of other countries, so that he might be in a position to render greater services to his own in the office to which he had been appointed. On this occasion he visited all the mines in Saxony and the Hartz mountains, and was royally entertained by Duke Ludvic Rudolf of Brunswick-Lüneburg, who showed him a generosity which he doubtless appreciated after his father's parsimony. Meanwhile his pen was by no means idle. He published a treatise at Amsterdam on Chemistry and Physics; some observations on Iron and Fire; and a work on the construction of Docks and Dykes; and later on, at Leipzig, some miscellaneous observations on Geology and Mineralogy. On his return home he settled down again for a period to his work at the Board of Mines, in the meantime gathering matter for further publications which followed in due course. The most important of these were his *Opera Philosophia Mineralia*, and a treatise on *The Infinite*. The former work met with a very favourable reception, and between one publication and another Swedenborg soon won for himself a European reputation. The Academy of Sciences at St Petersburg nominated him a corresponding member, while he was one of the first to be elected for the newly established Royal Academy of Sciences in his own country.

Everything thus seemed to open out for Swedenborg a career of great scientific and practical utility. He became, however, gradually led by his philosophical speculations to an investigation of the nature of the soul and its operation in the body, and the mutual relations of the two. This study was the subject of two important works, entitled respectively *The Economy of the Animal Kingdom considered Anatomically and Philosophically*, and *The Animal Kingdom considered Anatomically*,

EMANUEL SWEDENBORG

Physically, and Philosophically. By the "animal kingdom" must be understood the kingdom presided over by the soul. In the first of these books Swedenborg deals with the composition of the blood and its circulation, with the heart, arteries, and veins, and with the brain and its cortices. In this book Swedenborg attaches "great importance to the blood, for, as he says, nothing exists in the body that has not previously existed in the blood." He describes it again as "a vital and most spirituous fluid, which has an immediate connection with the soul." In the *Animal Kingdom* Swedenborg describes in full detail all the organs of the body and their uses, the object being in the end to track the soul home and to describe its activities. "For as yet," he tells us, "her modes of being and her nature are absolutely unknown." Naturally he recognises that this will be regarded by the philosophers of his day as a vain and useless quest. But he is prepared to meet their objections with the following pertinent remarks, which, now that the materialistic hypothesis has been finally discarded by the advance guard of modern Science, are likely to find a sympathetic echo in scientific as well as philosophic circles.

Inasmuch [he says] as the soul is the model, the idea, the first form, the substance, the force, and the principle of her organic body, and of all its forces and powers, or what amounts to the same thing, as the organic body is the image and type of its soul conformed and principled to the whole nature of the soul's efficiency, it follows that the one is represented in the other. . . . Thus by the body we are instructed respecting the soul, by the soul respecting the body, and by both respecting the truth of the whole.

Emerson describes the *Animal Kingdom* as "an anatomist's account of the human body in the highest style of poetry," and its object as to "put science and the soul, long estranged from each other, at one again." It was while continuing his pursuit of this apparently visionary aim that Swedenborg quite unexpectedly found himself, as he believed, in touch with another than the physical world. In writing of this extraordinary development in his life history in the Introduction to the *Arcana Cœlestia*, the first volume of which appeared in 1749, he gives his own account of his relationship with the spiritual realm in justification of the remarkably dogmatic statements contained in the book in question.

"It is," he says, "expedient here to premise that of the Lord's divine mercy it has been granted me now for several years to be constantly and uninterruptedly in company with spirits and angels, hearing them converse with each other and conversing with them. Hence it has been permitted me to hear and see things in another life which are astonishing, and which have never before come to the knowledge of any man nor entered into his imagination. I have thus been instructed concerning different kinds of spirits and the state of souls after death—concerning Hell, or the lamentable state of the unfaithful—concerning Heaven, or the most happy state of the faithful—and particularly concerning the doctrine of Faith, which is acknowledged throughout all Heaven, on which subjects, by the divine mercy of the Lord, more will be said in the following pages." With regard to the extraordinary transformation which these experiences brought about in his life's work, he explains to a friend that the Lord has elected him for this work, and " for revealing the spiritual meaning of the Sacred Scriptures which he had promised to the Prophets and in the Book of Revelation." " My purpose previously," he adds, " had been to explore Nature, chemistry, and the sciences of mining and anatomy."

The basis of Swedenborg's teaching which, of course, under the circumstances he did not claim in any way as original, was that the Bible must be accepted absolutely as a divinely inspired book, but must be taken in an allegorical sense. Thus where historical events are recorded they are not recorded for the sake of history, for the object of the Scriptures is to treat not of the kingdoms of the earth, but of the Kingdom of God. In other parts of the Bible, as in Genesis, there is no truth in the story from the historical point of view. The record is merely an allegory of the soul.

His doctrine of Correspondences was merely the recognition of this allegorical relationship of the spiritual and material. The universe, according to Swedenborg, is symbolical throughout. All material things are derived from their spiritual archetypes, and are representations of these. The bodily form represents the spiritual character, for the spirit forms the body in its own likeness. A man's acts are thus the outcome of his inward nature, and there is consequently a similar correspondence between them and the inward man. The basis of these ideas is, of course, the ancient occult teaching that the universe is the macrocosm, and man the microcosm. Thus Swedenborg tells us that as there is a material sun, moon, and stars, so each of these heavenly bodies has its mental and spiritual counterpart.

Swedenborg's doctrine of Degrees appears to follow from his doctrine of Correspondences. The three degrees of the human mind correspond to the three kingdoms of Nature : animal, vegetable, and mineral, corresponding to spirit, soul, and body. " Degrees," Swedenborg tells us, " are of two kinds, discrete and continuous." " All things, from least to greatest, in both the spiritual and natural worlds, co-exist at once from discrete and continuous degrees. In respect of discrete degrees there can be no intercourse between either by continuity." It follows, therefore, with regard to the degrees of the human mind, the celestial, spiritual, and the natural, that they cannot communicate under normal conditions one with another. Thus, too, men on earth can have no sensible communication with the spiritual world or see things of that world without a special opening of the spiritual sight. Elsewhere Swedenborg tells us "to the intent that anything may be perfect it must be distinguished into three degrees. The ground and reason of this is because there must be end, cause, and effect." Another doctrine of Swedenborg's was that of regeneration. In order to be partaker of the higher life, man, he held, must be born again, but this regeneration was not a special occurrence of any particular date, but a continuous process. One of the orthodox doctrines which Swedenborg attacked was that of the Trinity. He denied that Jesus Christ was merely the Second Person of a Divine Trinity. He cites St Paul's statement that "in Him dwelleth all the fullness of the Godhead bodily," and maintains that the whole Trinity is centred in his Person. "In consequence," he says, "of separating the Divine Trinity into Three Persons each of which is declared to be God and

Lord, a sort of frenzy has infected the whole system of theology as well as the Christian Church so called from its Divine Founder. . . . That a trinity of gods occupies the minds of Christians, although they deny it from shame, is very evident from the ingenuity of many who contrive methods to prove that three are one, and one three, by geometry, arithmetic, and physics. . . . Others have trifled with the Divine Trinity as jugglers play one with another. Their juggling on this subject may be compared to those sick of a fever who see a single object, such as a man, a table, or a candle, as three ; or three as one."

The basis of this orthodox Christian teaching with regard to the Trinity is, of course, the Athanasian Creed, which attempts to explain the matter by the absurd method of a juxtaposition of contradictions. It is well to bear in mind, in view of the enormous amount of theological twaddle that has been talked on this subject, that the Athanasian Creed was in the nature of a political concordat to meet the exigencies of a time of acute religious difficulty, and in no sense an exposition of spiritual truth.

As the orthodox doctrine of the Trinity was false, argued Swedenborg, and there were no three Persons, as supposed, it was, of course, impossible for one of them, the Son, to offer Himself as sacrifice to appease the wrath of another, the Father. The doctrine of the atonement, therefore, as taught by the Church, had no basis in fact. God needed no reconciliation to His creatures. It was they who needed to be reconciled to Him before they could be fitted to appear in His presence. Christ took upon Himself human nature that He might conquer mankind's spiritual enemies which were keeping him in bondage and estranged from his Divine Source.

One of Swedenborg's most astounding statements had reference to the Last Judgment. This was not, maintained Swedenborg, as the orthodox generally hold, the final consummation of all things. The event was an occurrence in the spiritual sphere which actually took place in the year 1757 ! It appears from this amazing account that in the Intermediate State so many undesirable and evil spiritual entities had accumulated that they were threatening the whole world with imminent catastrophe. It may be remembered, in this connection, that in Swedenborg's time scepticism was everywhere rampant, and that religious life had reached its lowest ebb. This was the case not only on the Continent, but pre-eminently in England, where the movement headed by John Wesley led to such remarkable scenes in connection with the great spiritual revival which followed this period of religious apathy. To avert the catastrophe threatened to the world according to Swedenborg's theory, a general judgment was executed upon the spirits who were in revolt and were imperilling the divine order. These powers of evil were at that date placed under restraint, so that an influx of new spiritual forces among men might be made possible. Swedenborg actually goes so far as to affirm that he himself was permitted to witness this judgment in fulfilment of the prophecies made in the Gospels and in the Book of Revelation.

The Swedenborgian teaching which has come in probably for most criticism is that with regard to Marriage. Swedenborg (thus far as it appears to me quite rightly) insisted that sex is a spiritual as well as a physical distinction. He denied the virtues of celibacy and declared that true chastity resides in the perfect marriage relation. Marriage, according to Swedenborg, is not a physical relationship till death part the united pair, but is eternal in its character. " Conjugial love " being the central and fundamental love of man's life is also the source of his fullest joy. The delights of the true conjugial love exceed the delights of all other loves. All delights that are felt by man proceed from love, and it follows, therefore, that the principal happiness in the celestial life must have a similar source, and the highest joy of heaven must therefore be the spiritual counterpart of the conjugial life of earth. It does not, of course, necessarily follow from this that earthly marriages are perpetuated in heaven. If the feelings of the marriage partners towards one another are concordant and sympathetic, they continue indeed their married life ; but if they are discordant and antipathetic, they dissolve it. For true conjugial love is the only possible form of marriage in heaven, and "as their love lasts to eternity, it follows that the wife becomes more and more a wife and the husband more and more a husband. The true reason of this is that in a marriage of truly conjugial love each married partner becomes continually a more interior man. For that love opens the interiors of their minds and in the proportion in which these are opened the man becomes more and more a man."

Swedenborg has some very beautiful observations with regard to the rejuvenescence of those who have passed into the higher life. "All who come into heaven," he says, "return into their vernal youth, and remain so to eternity. The more thousands of years they live the more beautiful and happy is the spring to which they attain. . . . In a word, to grow old in heaven is to grow young. . . . They who live in the chaste life of marriage are above all others in the order and form of Heaven after death. Their beauty, therefore, is surpassing, and the flower of their youth endures for ever."

What are we to say of this man who propounded this amazing gospel as a direct message from the highest spheres ? What are we to say of his communications and conversations with the unseen world ? Of his *bona fides* it is impossible to entertain a doubt. The ordinary hypothesis is that he suffered from hallucinations. It has been argued on the other hand, that for a man so sane and so shrewd in the ordinary affairs of the world, hallucinations of the kind were an impossibility. This, however, seems going rather too far. Some of the sanest men in the world have had special points on which they were not mentally sound. Monomania is a recognised form of mental aberration, and the man who suffers from it is as sane as his fellows on all matters except one.

This spiritual communion, however, was continuous in the case of Swedenborg for many years, and during those years occupied either in itself or in the activities that arose from it the larger portion of his life. In spite of this absorption, his relations with his fellow men continued as sane and responsible as those of any of his neighbours. Would this have been possible, one may ask, in the face of so absorbing an interest, had this interest merely been founded on a monomania ?

It would, I think, be difficult to parallel such a case. If, however, we decide to take Swedenborg's relations with the other world at his own valuation, are we called upon to accept his gospel at his own valuation on that account ? Certainly I think not. Swedenborg's estimate of the status of the spiritual beings with whom he communicated, even if we accept their reality, need not be ours. Recent investigations and records of innumerable psychic experiences have tended to show what a miscellaneous crowd of spirits hover around the confines of this material world. Swedenborg's mistake has been made by many spiritualists of the present day, and sometimes with disastrous results. Swedenborg had not before him the evidence which we now hold to warn him of the necessity of testing the quality of his spiritual communicants. The experiences encountered overwhelmed him by their unexpected and apparently miraculous character, and his naturally sane judgment was at fault for want of a criterion by which to estimate them.[1] Few of those who now accept the genuineness of psychical phenomena are prepared to question Swedenborg's exceptional mediumistic powers. To

[1] There are not a few of the communications recorded, notably in the "Spiritual Diary," which might be advanced to support the hypothesis of a disordered brain ; and we must not lose sight of the fact that Swedenborg's tireless activities taxed his intellectual faculties beyond the powers of any but the most exceptional human organism.

allow them to their fullest extent is by no means to accept the doctrine which was preached through his mediumship.

Of Swedenborg's psychic gifts there is indeed plenty of evidence quite outside the teachings of his celestial visitors. On one occasion he disclosed to the Queen of Sweden a secret that had existed between her and her deceased brother, the Crown Prince Augustus William of Prussia, which was unknown to any living person. On another he described to a whole company of people at Gothenburg a destructive fire which had broken out at that very moment in Stockholm. Again on another occasion he revealed to the widow of Monsieur de Marteville the hiding place of a missing receipt for money which had been paid by her husband, the Dutch Ambassador at Stockholm. These incidents are among the best authenticated of any extant historical records of a psychic character. The philosopher Kant, among others, made a searching investigation into the evidence on which they rested, and came away absolutely convinced of their truth. It is curious to note that John Wesley was not a little interested in the Swedenborgian propagandism. The great Methodist preacher was impressed with a strong desire to meet the Swedish seer—a desire to which, however, he had never given open expression. The Rev. Samuel Smith, one of Wesley's preachers, records how, about the end of February 1772 he was in attendance upon John Wesley, when the latter received a communication as follows from Swedenborg, who was then in London, which he read aloud.

GREAT BATH STREET,
GREAT BATH FIELDS.

SIR,—I have been informed in the world of spirits that you have a strong desire to converse with me. I shall be happy to see you if you will favour me with a visit. I am, sir, your humble servant,
EMANUEL SWEDENBORG.

Mr Wesley wrote in reply that he was then on the point of starting for a six months' journey, but would be pleased to wait on Swedenborg after his return to London. Swedenborg replied to this, that the visit proposed by Wesley would be too late, as he, Swedenborg, would enter the world of spirits on the 29th day of the next month, never more to return, a prediction which proved perfectly correct.

Other men have written many books. It is Swedenborg's unique distinction, if distinction it is, to be the one man in history who has written a library on his own account. The encyclopædic brain does not, as a rule, tend to perspicuity in style, and Swedenborg has suffered from neglect owing to the fact that the fertility of his genius was not sufficiently associated with the powers of selection and condensation. To search for the treasures of his knowledge among his published works is like looking, in the words of the hackneyed proverb, "for needles in a haystack." Had he given us far less in volume the world would doubtless have profited more by the very valuable information contained in his writings.

There are times when one is inclined to regret (if also to feel thankfulness) that Swedenborg was side-tracked by his Celestials and that he did not complete his phenomenal career on the lines which he had marked out for himself. It is a vain, though a most alluring speculation, to consider how the destinies of nations might have evolved if certain incidents in a single life history had eventuated otherwise than they did. We may conceive of Swedenborg bringing to completion his schemes for the construction of flying machines and submarines, nearly two centuries earlier than was decreed by destiny, and ask ourselves, if we will, what use the great Napoleon might not have made of these formidable implements of destructive warfare, and how far the map of Europe, and indeed of the world, might have been changed through their employment by his formidable genius ; or, again, to what extent the linking up of the New and Old Worlds might have been accelerated by such developments.

Here at least we must admit was a phenomenon—
a man who realised, in a measure undreamed of
by his contemporaries, not only in the physical
but also in the spiritual sphere, the stupendous
possibilities of the Coming Time.

VI

COUNT CAGLIOSTRO

WHO has not heard of Cagliostro ? And yet who but a few students have any real knowledge of that mysterious character, of whom it may be said, as it was of Melchizedek, that he had " neither beginning of life nor end of days." Both, at least, like the king of Salem's, are wrapped in uncertainty, and though popular tradition, repeated again and again by the uncritical historian, has identified Cagliostro's early life with that of the Italian scoundrel Joseph Balsamo, the evidence is as near conclusive as presumptive evidence can well be, that the two had no connection whatever with one another, beyond having married Italian wives with the same surname [1]—and that by no means an uncommon one—and the fact that Balsamo is said to have had an uncle of the name of Cagliostro. From what we know of Balsamo it may fairly be

[1] The Christian name of Balsamo's wife was Lorenza, of Cagliostro's Seraphina. But the story is itself of doubtful authenticity.

said that two people more opposite in character than himself and Count Cagliostro would be difficult to discover, and the identification of the two would seem to involve the assumption that Cagliostro had discarded his first wife and taken a second, a supposition which would render worthless the argument based on the identity of their surnames.

Cagliostro's whole career, as far as we know it, shows a character in which generosity is perpetually being carried to the verge of folly. His credulity was constantly making him the dupe of designing knaves, in whose honesty he placed a pathetic faith, and had he ever had the misfortune to encounter his alter ego, a common rogue of the most ordinary type, it is safe to predict that he would not have escaped from his clutches till he had been fleeced of the bulk of his possessions. As late as the date of his trial in the affair of the Diamond Necklace, no suggestion of the identity of the two characters was even mooted. The story owes its origin to the fertile brain of one of the greatest scoundrels of whom European history holds record, the notorious blackmailer, Theveneau de Morande.

A short *résumé* of this arch-villain's history will probably be sufficient to dissipate any credence which has ever been placed in a narrative for which his assertions are our only authority. Theveneau de Morande was born in 1741, the son of a lawyer, at Arnay-le-Duc, in Burgundy. As a boy he was arrested for theft in a house of ill-fame. Subsequently he enlisted, obtained his discharge through his father's intervention, found himself once more in prison at For-l'Evêque, and was then confined in a convent at Armentières, from which he was released two years after at the age of four-and-twenty. Having shortly after lampooned one of the members of the government, he was compelled to fly the country and took refuge in England, where he arrived in a state of destitution.

Needs must when the devil drives, and, the pinch of poverty sharpening his wits, he now turned his attention to the black-mailing business, in the pursuit of which he was soon to evince a quite uncommon aptitude and adroitness. His talents in this direction were ably seconded by a facile pen and a command of vituperative language and personal abuse which the author of the Letters of Junius could scarcely have outdone. His first effort of importance in this direction was *Le Gazetier Cuirassé, ou Anecdotes Scandaleuses sur la Cour de France*. Those who would not purchase immunity by a lump sum down had their characters and private lives mercilessly torn to pieces in its pages. The book is said to have brought him £1000. An attempt to blackmail Voltaire was less successful. The veteran *philosophe* published the blackmailer's

To face p. 122

COUNT CAGLIOSTRO
From an engraving by Bartolozzi, in the British Museum.

letter with comments by his own satiric pen. The blackmailer's path has indeed its ups and downs, and once he was fain to accept a horsewhipping and publish an abject apology, the price extorted by an offended French nobleman. Madame du Barry, however, Louis XV.'s notorious favourite, was made of other stuff, and in consequence the *Memoires d'une Femme Publique*, compared with which *Le Gazetier Cuirassé* was said to have been "rosewater," were never published. Morande accepted the sum of 32,000 livres in solatium for his wounded literary *amour propre*. Before, however, paying him his price the French Government had attempted to kidnap the audacious libeller. This was the ancient substitute for the more prosaic extradition methods of modern times. The plot, however, failed. With a dexterity worthy of a better cause, Morande, warned in time, was able to pose in the English press as a political exile and avenger of public morality. The sympathy of the susceptible public responded warmly to the unscrupulous appeal, and the representatives of French authority escaped with difficulty from the clutches of an infuriated London mob.

It not unfrequently happens with countries that have been at war, that the signature of the treaty of peace is followed after no long lapse of time by a formal alliance between the erstwhile foes, there being obviously two methods of gaining one's ends, the method of grab and the method of give and take, and the failure of one suggesting the advisability of adopting the other. So at least reasoned the French Government, and the payment of Morande's price was followed in due course by his employment on behalf of the said Government in the capacity of subsidised journalist, and spy. Morande was nothing loth to come to terms, and eventually blossomed out into the Editor of the *Courier de l'Europe*. This journal, originally started by Latour under the ægis of the French Government, was soon read in every corner of the Continent. This was the weapon which of all others the blackmailer desired for his purposes. "In it," says Brisset, "he tore to pieces the most estimable people, and manufactured, or caused to be manufactured, articles to ruin any one whom he feared."

Cagliostro had — all unwittingly — made dire enemies of the French Court through his acquittal in the trial over the Diamond Necklace affair. To acquit Cagliostro, who had no more to do with the matter in question than the man in the moon, appeared from the royal standpoint to be tantamount to incriminating the Queen, on whom, in fact, suspicion long and not unnaturally rested. Morande, therefore, received his instructions from Paris to ruin Cagliostro's reputation. The means ready to his hand was the *Courier de l'Europe*. Hence the story of Joseph Balsamo and his identification with the *soi-disant* Count Cagliostro. To say that the authority hardly seems adequate is surely to put it mildly. And yet Carlyle, and others before and after him, have quietly accepted the statement of the paid blackmailer as sufficient evidence of the character and history of his victim!

Who, then, was Cagliostro? The answer to this question must ever remain among the unsolved problems of history. There is, however, no reason to dismiss as incredible—even if there is reason to doubt—the account which he gave of himself on the occasion of the "Diamond Necklace" trial. From what we know of Cagliostro we may, I think, say that his character was far too ingenuous for him to have been likely to invent so remarkable a tale. Everything, however, in his history points to the fact that he was just the person to take a record of the kind and colour it with the hues of his own fertile imagination. In any case, the impartial historian, while dismissing as preposterous the Balsamo fiction is bound to give some weight—however slight—to the only evidence on the subject we possess which is not manifestly untrue. Cagliostro, however, himself did not pretend to have knowledge of his parentage. "I cannot," he states, "speak positively as to the place of my nativity, nor as to the parents who gave me birth. All my inquiries have ended only in giving me some great notions, it is true, but altogether vague and uncertain, concerning my family." The gist, however, of his story was that he spent his childhood in Arabia, where he was brought up under the name of Acherat. He had then, he states, four persons attached to his service—the chief of whom was a certain Althotas, a man between fifty-five and sixty years of age. This man (whom it has been attempted to identify with a certain Kölmer, a Jutland merchant, who had travelled extensively and had the reputation of being a master-magician) informed Cagliostro that he had been left an orphan when three months old, and that his parents were Christian and nobly born. All his attempts, however, to discover the secret of his birth were doomed to disappointment. The matter was one which was treated as taboo. In his twelfth year (to follow his own story) he left Medina for Mecca, where he remained three years, until, wearying of the monotonous round of the Cherif's Court, he obtained leave to travel.

One day (he narrates), when I was alone, the prince entered my apartment; he strained me to his bosom with more than usual tenderness, bid me never cease to adore the Almighty, and added, bedewing my cheeks with his tears : " Nature's unfortunate child, adieu ! "

From this date commenced, according to his

own account, Cagliostro's travels, first in company with Althotas, for whom he ever expressed the warmest affection, afterwards with the wife whom he chose for himself in Italy. For upwards of three years he claims to have travelled through Egypt, Africa, and Asia, finally reaching the island of Rhodes in the year 1766, and thence embarking on a French ship bound for Malta. Here he and his guardian were received with all honour, Pinto, the Grand Master of the Knights of Malta, giving them apartments in his palace.

It was here (he notes) that I first assumed European dress and with it the name of Count Cagliostro ; nor was it a small matter of surprise to me to see Althotas appear in a clerical dress with the insignia of the Order of Malta.

The Grand Master Pinto was apparently acquainted with Cagliostro's history. He often spoke to him, he says, of the Cherif, but always refused to be " drawn " on the subject of his real origin and birth. He treated him, however, with every consideration and endeavoured to induce him to " take the cross," promising him a great career and rapid preferment if he would consent to do so. Cagliostro's love of travelling and of the study of medicine drew him in another direction, and on the death of his guardian, Althotas, which occurred shortly after, he left Malta for ever. After visiting Sicily and the Greek Archipelago in company with the

Chevalier d'Aquino he proceeded thence to Naples, where he took leave of his companion. Provided with a letter of credit on the banking house of Signor Bellone he left Naples for Rome, where his destiny awaited him in the shape of Seraphina Feliciani, who shortly after became his wife, and to whom he showed throughout his married life a most unfailing devotion.[1] Cagliostro states that he was then (anno 1770) in his twenty-second year, and he appears to have continued to pursue that nomadic life which was so dear to him, travelling from town to town on the Continent of Europe till he at length emerges into the light of day in the city of London, in the month of July 1776, in furnished apartments in Whitcombe Street, Leicester Fields. London seems always to have been an unfortunate place for Cagliostro, and here he was destined, on the first of many occasions, to become the victim of his own too trustful and generous disposition and to be fleeced of the greater part of his possessions by a nest of rogues, who took advantage of a foreigner entirely ignorant of London. Eventually he was rescued from this gang of knaves by a good Samaritan in the shape of a certain O'Reilly. Now O'Reilly was a prominent member of the Esperance Lodge of Freemasons, and here we first

[1] It is perhaps almost superfluous to state that Joseph Balsamo got his wife locked up in jail, beside compelling her to lead a life of immorality.

find Cagliostro brought into contact with that celebrated secret society, his connection with which was destined to play so all-important a part in the subsequent years of his life. O'Reilly, it appears, was the proprietor of the *King's Head*, in Gerard Street, where the Esperance Lodge assembled, and it was only natural that one so fascinated with the occult as Cagliostro should be readily persuaded by his benefactor and rescuer to become initiated into the order of Freemasons. It is not necessary here to follow in detail the sordid intrigues of which, during his sojourn in England, he was made the victim. He was, however, glad eventually to escape from the country, with " no more than £50 and some jewels " in his possession, having lost in all, through fraud and consequent legal proceedings, some 3000 guineas during his sojourn. Cagliostro's star, however, had not yet set, and his all too brief spell of fame and triumph was still in front of him. Providence, in the shape probably of the emissaries of Freemasonry, was waiting at Brussels to replenish his purse, and the same Providence, probably in the same guise, replenished it many times afterwards with no niggardly hand.

From Brussels to The Hague, from The Hague to Nuremberg, from Nuremberg to Berlin, from Berlin to Leipzig, we trace the Count's peregrinations, gathering fame and founding Egyptian

Masonic Lodges as he went. It is true he met with setbacks and reverses, and the capital of Frederick the Great would have none of him, but it is clear that, in spite of these, his credit and reputation as a healer and clairvoyant grew steadily in volume. It was, in fact, on these two gifts that his fame rested. Though he claimed to have been taught the secrets of occultism by Althotas, or to have learned them from the Egyptian priests, there is no evidence [1] throughout the records of his career of his possessing anything but a smattering of such abstruse knowledge, and on several occasions, notably at St Petersburg, there is something more than a suspicion that his attempt to make good his claim to the name of occultist involved him in serious humiliation and rebuffs. The tales, however, of his predictions and their fulfilments were handed on from mouth to mouth, doubtless losing nothing on the way, while his reputation as a healer and the stories of the cures which he effected assured a perfect furore of enthusiasm in every fresh town to which he paid a visit. He took advantage of this enthusiasm to found fresh Masonic Lodges in all directions, and, while he consistently refused to receive payment of any kind for his cures, the shekels of an endless file of initiate converts poured

[1] Unless indeed we accept the (doubtful) story of his transmuting metals for De Rohan.

into the coffers at the headquarters of Egyptian Masonry. Never was man at once more lavish with money and more indifferent to the comforts which money brings. "He slept in an armchair," said Madame d'Oberkirch contemptuously, "and lived on cheese." Whatever he spent, however, he appeared to draw from an inexhaustible widow's cruise. As in spite of his refusal to accept fees, he paid his own bills with the greatest promptitude; the problem whence this continuous stream of gold flowed excited unbounded curiosity, and many were the fantastic stories invented to account for it.

Meanwhile, after visiting Mittau, where he was enthusiastically taken up by Marshal von Medem, the head of the Masonic Lodge at that place, he passed on to Petersburg, Warsaw, and thence to Strassburg. Here he was destined to enjoy a great triumph and to win a powerful friend, who was eventually, through a pure accident, to prove the cause of his undoing. This was none other than the notorious Cardinal de Rohan. It is hardly necessary to state that the ecclesiastical dignitary of the eighteenth century in France was not selected for his high office by reason of his exemplary life or his Christian virtues. To neither of these did Cardinal de Rohan make any claim. Yet honours had fallen thick and fast upon him. He was Bishop of Strassburg, Grand Almoner of France, Cardinal,

Prince of the Empire, Landgrave of Alsace, in addition to being Abbot of the richest abbey in France, the Abbey of St Waast Handsune. Of fascinating manner, an aristocrat of the aristocrats, there was no position in the kingdom to which he did not feel justified in aspiring. The fact that he enjoyed a reputation for dissipation and extravagance did not appear calculated to tell against him in such an age.

Surprising as it may seem, the Cardinal combined with a pleasure-loving disposition a passion for alchemy and the pursuit of the occult sciences, and the arrival of Cagliostro at Strassburg naturally enough excited his interest to no small degree. The Cardinal determined to lose no time in making the acquaintance of the man about whom and whose marvellous cures the whole town was already talking almost before he set foot in its streets. But Cagliostro was inclined to ride the high horse. "If the Cardinal is ill," he replied to the great man's messenger, "let him come to me and I will cure him. If not, he has no need of me nor I of him." In spite of the Count's stand-offishness, the Cardinal was not to be denied, and the acquaintance once made soon ripened into the closest intimacy. Cagliostro was told to consider the palace his own, and he and his wife resided there on the footing of the most honoured guests. Marvellous tales are told of the results of his experiments in the Cardinal's laboratory, how he manufactured gold and jewels, and finally showed De Rohan in the crystal the form of the woman whom he had loved. It is on these stories alone that the reputation of Cagliostro as an alchemist really rests, and in the absence of further confirmatory evidence one is inclined to take them with a grain of salt. However this may be, it is certain that the Cardinal was completely won over, and Cagliostro took care not to lose caste by assuming airs of humility or deference. Never, certainly, was there less of a snob than this marvellous adventurer. "Cagliostro," says Madame d'Oberkirch, "treated him and his other distinguished admirers as if they were under the deepest obligation to him; but he under none whatever to them." As usual, our hero was besieged at Strassburg by those who would profit by his medical knowledge and skill as a healer, for he really appears to have possessed both, and as usual by obliging his clients he incurred the inveterate hostility of the medical profession. In all ages of the world's history the natural healer has had the doctor as his enemy, and the prophet, the priest. Orthodoxy has ever closed its ranks against those who poach on its preserves. Doubtless it is the natural instinct of self-defence. For Cagliostro, however, it was extremely inconvenient.

The people would throng his doorsteps to be cured and make him heal them willy-nilly, and the medical profession were equally determined to make each place in which he practised his medical skill too hot for him. Others might have been willing to let the dogs bark, but a fatal sensitiveness to criticism made the Count an all too easy target for their venom. They drove him from Strassburg as they had driven him from other places, in spite of the entreaties of De Rohan, who pressed him to stay and disregard their clamour.

We need not follow Cagliostro from Strassburg to Bordeaux and from Bordeaux to Lyons, where he added further laurels to his reputation and founded further Lodges of Egyptian Masonry. He might have remained indefinitely to all appearance at the latter place if it had not been for the solicitations of Cardinal de Rohan, who urged him to respond to the appeals of Parisian Society and visit the gay capital, where he guaranteed him an enthusiastic reception. He even sent a special messenger to back his request, and perhaps Cagliostro himself had heard the capital of cultured Europe a-calling. Anyhow he came, his evil fate—if not Paris— summoning him. Cagliostro declared that he took the greatest precaution on arriving there to avoid causing ill-will. However this may be, he immediately became "the rage" in fashionable circles; people flocked to him by hundreds to be cured, and the stories of the miracles which he was supposed to have effected were the talk of every dinner-party in the capital. Mesmer had already left Paris with a fortune of 340,000 livres, made by his lucrative practice, in his pocket. Paris, craving for a new excitement, was ready to receive with open arms the wonder-worker of whom it was said that no one of all his patients ever succeeded in making him accept the least mark of gratitude.[1]

Cagliostro was here surfeited with flattery. Houdin executed his bust. His statuettes were in every shop window. His portrait was in every house. Those who claimed to have been cured by him were met with on all sides. Angels, it is said, and heroes of Biblical story appeared at his séances. No story was too absurd for Paris to believe about him.

But a train of events in which he had no hand, and a catastrophe for which he had no responsibility, were destined, while wrecking other reputations and undermining the throne itself, to bring his career of triumph to a sudden and tragic close, and eventually to drive him, a forsaken and persecuted outcast, to his final doom. Cagliostro, as already stated, had nothing whatever to do with the affair

[1] Grimm.

of the Diamond Necklace. But for all that, he was caught in the web of deceit that an unscrupulous woman had woven to suit her own purposes.

The Countess de Lamotte-Valois, a descendant of a natural son of Henri II., and an adventuress of the most reckless type, had found a protector in the person of the susceptible Cardinal de Rohan. Now the Cardinal was by no means a *persona grata* at the Court of Versailles. As a matter of fact, he was never seen there except at the feast of the Assumption, when it was his duty as Grand Almoner to celebrate Mass in the Royal Chapel. The cause of this was the enmity of Queen Marie Antoinette. The Cardinal had been recalled from the embassy at Vienna at the instance of her mother, Maria Theresa, and doubtless the mother had communicated to the daughter a distrust for the brilliant but pleasure-loving Cardinal. This was a fatal obstacle to De Rohan, whose ambition it was to become First Minister to the King. The Countess de Lamotte saw her chance in the thwarted ambitions of her protector, and took care to pose as an intimate friend of the Queen, a story to which her frequent visits to Versailles in connection with a petition for the recovery of some family property which had passed into the possession of the State, lent a certain appearance of truth. She represented to the Cardinal the interest the Queen took in him but which matters of policy compelled her to dissemble. In the sequel, a series of letters—of course forged—passed between De Rohan and the supposed Queen. The Queen, through the intermediary of the Countess, borrowed large sums of money of the Cardinal, which the Cardinal, on his part, being head over ears in debt in spite of his enormous income, was compelled to borrow of the Jews. Then, when the Cardinal was becoming suspicious, the Countess arranged a bogus interview, at which another lady—admittedly remarkably like her—posed as the Queen, and permitted De Rohan to kiss her hand. Finally, Madame de Lamotte got in touch with Böhmer, the owner of the famous necklace. This she represented to the Cardinal that the Queen had set her heart on obtaining, but could not, at a moment's notice, find the ready cash. Would he become security? Needless to say, De Rohan fell into the trap. The first instalment of the bill fell due, and the Cardinal, who had not expected to be called on to pay, was unable offhand to find the money. At this point Böhmer, feeling nervous, consulted one of the Queen's ladies-in-waiting, who informed him that the story of the Queen having bought the necklace was all moonshine. He then went to the Countess de Lamotte, who had the effrontery to say she believed he was being victimised, and advised him to go to the Cardinal, thinking, doubtless, that De Rohan would take the entire responsibility when the alternative was his ruin. The jeweller, however, instead of taking her advice, went straight to the King. The King immediately communicated with the Queen, who was furious, and insisted on having the Cardinal arrested forthwith. The fat was now in the fire with a vengeance. The arrest of the Cardinal was followed by that of the Countess de Lamotte, of Cagliostro and his wife (whom the Countess in utter recklessness accused of the theft of the necklace), of the Baroness d'Oliva, who had "played" the Queen, of de Vilette, the forger of the letters, and various minor actors in this astounding drama.

In the celebrated trial that followed Cagliostro was acquitted, but not until he had spent nine months in the Bastille. There was, in fact, not a shadow of evidence against him. His wife was released before the trial took place. Cagliostro received an ovation from the people of Paris on the occasion of his release, as well as De Rohan, who was also acquitted, the popularity of the verdict being due to the hatred with which the Royal Family were now everywhere regarded. But on the day after, by a Royal edict, De Rohan was stripped of all his dignities and exiled to Auvergne, while Cagliostro was ordered to leave

France within three weeks. The Count retired to England, fearful lest worse might befall him; but even here the relentless malignity of the discredited Queen, who regarded his acquittal as equivalent to her own condemnation, followed his footsteps. The unscrupulous De Morande, as we have already seen, was paid by the Court to ruin his reputation and to identify him with the thief and gaolbird Joseph Balsamo. London was soon made so hot for him that he returned once more to the Continent, and made his home for a short time in Switzerland. Later on he went to Trent, where the Prince-Bishop, who had a passion for alchemy, made him a welcome guest. But the Count's day was over, and misfortune continued to dog his footsteps. The Emperor Joseph II. would not permit his vassal to harbour the man who had been mixed up in the Diamond Necklace affair, and the Bishop was reluctantly obliged to bid him begone. Cagliostro now found himself driven from pillar to post, his resources were at an end, and his friends were dead or had deserted him. He turned his steps towards Italy, and eventually arrived at Rome. Here his presence becoming known to the papal authorities, he and his wife were arrested as members of the Masonic Fraternity. In those days, within the Papal States Freemasonry was a crime punishable by death. After a mock trial the death-sentence was commuted to imprisonment for life, while his wife was confined in a penitentiary.

Rumour which wove a web of romance round all his doings, did not leave him even here, and stories were circulated that he had escaped from his dungeon and was living in Russia. There appears, however, to be no doubt that neither Count nor Countess long survived their incarceration, and when the French soldiers invaded the Papal States in 1797 and the Polish Legion under General Daubrowski captured the fortress of San Leo, in which the Count had been confined, the officers who inquired after the once famous magician, hoping to set him free, were informed that it was too late, and that he was already dead. The Queen, whose vindictive spite had ruined these two lives, went to her doom first ; but her instrument, the blackmailer Morande, retired to a quiet corner of France on his ill-gotten fortune, escaped the furies of the French Revolution, and ended his life surrounded by an atmosphere of the most unquestioned respectability.

And what of the man with whom not only his own fate, but the misrepresentations of history have dealt so hardly ? What manner of man was he for whom even those who denounce him as mountebank might not unreasonably, one would think, feel a passing sympathy ? On two points we have ample testimony. All those who knew him bore witness to the marvellous magnetism of his personality and to the fascination and beauty of his extraordinary eyes. " No two eyes like his were ever seen," says the Marquise de Crégny, " and his teeth were superb." " He was not, strictly speaking, handsome," says Madame d'Oberkirch, " but I have never seen a more remarkable face. His glance was so penetrating that one might almost be tempted to call it supernatural. I could not describe the expression of his eyes ; it was, so to speak, a mixture of flame and ice. It attracted and repelled at the same time, and, whilst it inspired terror, it aroused along with it an irresistible curiosity. I cannot deny," she adds, " that Cagliostro possessed an almost demoniacal power." Not less noteworthy is the opinion of so hostile a witness as Beugnot, who confesses, while ridiculing him, that his face, his attire, the whole man, in fact, impressed him in spite of himself. " If gibberish can be sublime," he continues, " Cagliostro was sublime. When he began speaking on a subject he seemed carried away with it, and spoke impressively in a ringing, sonorous voice."

This was the man whose appearance Carlyle caricatured in the following elegant phraseology :

A most portentous face of scoundrelism ; a fat snub abominable face ; dew-lapped, flat-nosed, greasy, full of greediness, sensuality, ox-like obstinacy; the most perfect quack face produced by the eighteenth century.

Carlyle, however, who would say anything or write anything in his moods of irritability, also alluded to the late Cardinal Newman as "not possessing the intellect of a moderate-sized rabbit"; and the two statements may fairly be juxtaposed.

Mr W. R. H. Trowbridge, to whose recent book I am greatly indebted for material for this brief sketch of Cagliostro's life, well observes that "there is perhaps no other equally celebrated personality in modern history whose character is so baffling to the biographer." History has condemned him purely on the evidence of his most unscrupulous enemies. But while dismissing such one-sided portraits, it is no easy matter to arrive at an unprejudiced valuation of the real man. Of his latest biographer's impartiality and candour, as well as his careful research of authorities, it is impossible to speak too highly. His conclusions will be all the more widely accepted in view of the fact that he is himself in no sense an occultist. In spite of a rather long chapter dealing with "Eighteenth Century Occultism," we feel instinctively and at every turn that the subject is one in which he is obviously out of his depth. Indeed, only on the second page of his biography we come across the following surprising statement. Speaking of "theosophists, spiritualists, occultists," all of whom are unceremoniously lumped together, he observes :

By these amiable visionaries Cagliostro is regarded as one of the princes of occultism whose mystical touch has revealed the arcana of the spiritual world to the initiated, and illumined the path along which the speculative scientist proceeds on entering the labyrinth of the supernatural.

Every occultist knows this to be sheer rubbish. Cagliostro has never been regarded as an authority in any school of occultism. Many, if not most occultists, have been inclined to believe that he was more than half a quack. Mr Trowbridge—it is to be said to his credit—has judged him in the light of the evidence more fairly than they. The truth is that, Cagliostro with all his good qualities, with all his generosity of heart, his human sympathy, his nobility—yes, it really was nobility—of character, was beyond and above all things a poser and a mystery-monger. He had a magnetic personality, a mediumistic temperament, and almost certainly some clairvoyant power, though it is noticeable that he invariably employed a little boy or girl whose assistance was essential to his predictions. Beyond this, and, I think we must say, more important than all this, he had an incontestable natural healing gift, which he aided by no small knowledge of practical medicine. In these qualifications we have the secret of his success, and also the clue to his failure. He was excessively vain, and loved to impress the multitude. He loved, moreover, to impress them by surrounding himself with an atmosphere of mystery and posing as an occultist, which (probably) he never was. He has left no body of teaching behind him. He has left no followers, no disciples. He was merely the comet of a season, though an exceptionally brilliant one. It would be absurd to class him in the same category as such master occultists as Cornelius Agrippa and Paracelsus, or indeed even as Eliphas Levi. He was not cast in the same mould. He belonged to another and a lower type. But his was withal a striking as well as a sympathetic personality, a personality that makes appeal, by a certain glamour heightened by the tragedy of his inglorious end, to all that is warm, and chivalrous, and romantic in the human heart.

VII

ANNA KINGSFORD AND EDWARD MAITLAND

WE are all of us familiar with the old proverb that marriages are made in Heaven, though there are few of us who believe it. It may, however, well be true that there are certain spiritual marriages or associations which are made in Heaven in the sense that they have a certain cosmic foundation in the nature of things and in the relationship of one life to another. It may also be true that two lives are brought together for special and important purposes by influences working from another and a far higher plane. Collaboration is a very commonplace word, but there was certainly no element of the commonplace in the collaboration of Anna Kingsford and Edward Maitland. History perhaps contains nothing more remarkable, and romance nothing more romantic, than this singular association of two strikingly diverse and original characters of opposite sexes for a single and supreme purpose. To the two individuals concerned, the sacrifice of two lives to the ideal which inspired them seemed but little in view of the momentous character of the objects to be achieved. The world may not set the same store on the high mission of Anna Kingsford and Edward Maitland, may not perhaps value it at the same price as the two co-workers who gave up their all in pursuit of their aims. Many may say, as many have said already, that, like Arthur's Knights of the Round Table, they were pursuing a will-o'-the-wisp and not the Holy Grail of their hearts' desire. But assuming that they partially misinterpreted the end to be achieved, or, alternatively, over-estimated their own powers of achieving that end with anything like the success that so high an ideal demanded, it should still be borne in mind that those who under-estimate the greatness of their own mission must inevitably fail to impress others with its value in the scheme of things, and it is therefore far better to over-estimate your own powers and the importance of the object aimed at than to underrate either the one or the other.

People are apt to look scoffingly at the man with a mission, but it is the men and the women with missions who have in fact made the world what it is to-day. "A crank," said some wit, "is a little thing that makes revolutions." The saying is as true as it was in the times of Jesus Christ, that God

To face p. 146

ANNA KINGSFORD

has "chosen the foolish things of the world to confound the wise, and the weak things of the world to confound the things which are mighty." If there is one word in our language more misunderstood than any other, it is the little word "Faith." We have been told by the cynical that faith is the capacity for believing that which we know to be untrue, and the misinterpretation of this term by the orthodox clergy is responsible for the derision which has been cast upon it. Worst of all sinners within the fold of the Church has been the evangelical contingent. "Believe," they tell us, "all the dry-as-dust dogmas of orthodox theology, and you will win eternal salvation." This is not, we may be sure, the sense in which Jesus used the word. Neither is it the sense in which, in a magnificently eloquent passage, the word was employed by the author of the Epistle to the Hebrews, when he spoke of those who "through faith subdued kingdoms, wrought righteousness, obtained promises, stopped the mouths of lions ; quenched the violence of fire, escaped the edge of the sword, out of weakness were made strong, waxed valiant in fight, and turned to flight the armies of the aliens."

The faith of Jesus and the faith of his apostles and followers is the faith that implies and includes the power to achieve. It is what we call in the ordinary language of the day "self-confidence," but it is not the confidence in the *lower* but in the *higher* self ; it is the confidence which comes of the conscious placing of ourselves *en rapport* with what Prentice Mulford called "the Infinite Life" and the "Divine Source." This power is the secret of all great achievement. The *faith* of the orthodox, on the other hand, corresponds to the *credulity* of the man in the street. It is the will-o'-the-wisp that leads fools to sacrifice the reality for a chimera. It was in condemnation and in ridicule of such folly as this that Omar Khayyám bade his friends "take the cash and let the credit go." It was in the spirit of this true self-confidence and self-reliance that Anna Kingsford and Edward Maitland entered upon the daring project of their life's work. It was this spirit of faith that enabled them to carry it at length to a triumphant conclusion—successful in spite of those imperfections inevitably incidental to a work of the kind, achieved under the defective conditions of present-day humanity.

A great work was certainly seldom, if ever, accomplished under such curious and such self-contradictory conditions. A man and a woman have frequently worked together before, and worked effectively and harmoniously, but they have either been in the relationship of husband and wife, of avowed lovers, independent of or having deliberately cast aside other ties, or they have been free to work together as friends owing to the fact that circumstances have left them unhampered by family conditions. The peculiarity of the present case is that the relations of Anna Kingsford and Edward Maitland subsisted in spite of the existence of a husband for whom his wife had a very genuine and warm affection, and who most undoubtedly reciprocated it to the full—in spite also of the fact that the husband was fully aware of, and approved of, all that took place, without seeing anything in it to lessen his esteem for his wife or compromise their relationship—in spite also of the fact that the society of the day held up its hands in horror at the scandal and more than suspected immorality where there was none to suspect—in spite, finally, of the fact that, joined to the respect and friendly feeling which Edward Maitland felt for the husband, there was something in his whole attitude and demeanour towards Anna Kingsford which was more in the nature of the devotion of a lover to his mistress than anything else which the ordinary terms of language can express. When Anna Kingsford passed away to another sphere early indeed in life (she was but forty-two), but with her life's work accomplished, the two who joined hands over her grave and who mourned her most deeply and most sincerely were the devoted husband who loved her without understanding the most remarkable side of her character, and the friend who loved and understood, but, better even than the woman whom he loved, loved the work of which her presence and being were to him the divine symbol and seal. People of the type of Anna Bonus Kingsford are too sensitive and impressionable ever to be really happy for long. The acuteness of their feelings exaggerates their own sufferings, and at the same time makes the consciousness of the sufferings of others an ever present torture and martyrdom. Mrs Kingsford's life, indeed, at times when her health, always far from robust, was below the usual level, became absolutely unbearable. The thought of bringing a child into the world to share her own anguish and despair seemed in itself a crime.

I long (she writes, in one of these moods of depression), I long for a little rest and peace. The world has grown very bitter to me. I feel as if every one were dead!

Ah, what a life is before me!—a life of incessant struggle, reproach, and loneliness. I shall never be as other women, happy in their wifehood and motherhood. Never to my dying day shall I know the meaning of a home.

And behind me, as I look back on the road by which I have come, all is storm and darkness. I fought my way through my lonely, sad-hearted childhood; I fought my way through my girlhood, misunderstood, and mistrusted always; and now, in my womanhood, I am fighting still. On every side of me are rebuke and suspicion, and bitter, abiding sorrow. Pain and suffering of body and of spirit have hung on my steps all the years of my life. I have had no respite.

Is there never to be peace? Never to be a time of sunlight that shall make me glad of my being?

Her spirit was indeed naked and without defence against the arrows of the world. Endowed with courage far greater than falls to the lot of most women, with great independence and an utter fearlessness of conventionality, she had no hesitation in avowing her own profound belief in her divine mission. To one who, meeting her for the first time, observed with ill-timed jocularity, "I understand, Mrs Kingsford, that you are a prophetess," she retorted with the utmost solemnity, "I am indeed a prophetess," and on her interrogator continuing his banter by inquiring: "But not, I suppose, as great as Isaiah?" "Yes," she returned, "greater than Isaiah." Such mockery, however boldly she faced it, caused her the most acute pain. There was, indeed, nothing undignified about her avowal of her claims, nothing that jarred, nothing of the charlatan in her composition. If she was deceived herself, at least she never dreamed of deceiving others. She never posed or attempted to gain a hearing by acting a part which was not natural to her. She was too genuine, too intense in her convictions, and withal too natural and too unaffected to be otherwise than always and everywhere true to herself. She was essentially a child of nature, and in some of the traits of her character she retained to the end the simplicity and wayward playfulness which most people say good-bye to when they reach years of discretion. Animals, of course, always appealed to her strongest sympathies, and for nine long years she could not bear to be parted except for occasional very brief periods from her favourite guinea-pig, Rufus. Nature in its varying moods made the strong appeal which it always does to people of so emotional a temperament. Once after recovering from a serious bout of illness she was taken to convalesce at Dieppe. An incident occurred here very illustrative of her susceptible nature. Having stayed for some time and being greatly benefited by the change, she was proceeding in company with Mr Edward Maitland to see her husband off by the steamer. Says her biographer:

It was a day of days for beauty. While waiting, we sat watching the gambols of a flock of sea-gulls, whose gleaming white wings, as they circled round and round against a sky of clearest and tenderest blue, approaching each other to give loving salute with their bills, and then darting off only to return and repeat the act, uttering the while shrill notes of joy and delight, made a spectacle of exquisite beauty, and one that went to the invalid's inmost heart, inducing an estatic sense of the possibilities of happiness in the mere fact of a natural and healthy existence. Though entranced by the scene no less than my companion, I did not fail to note the effect upon her, and the thought arose in my mind, " This is the best remedy of all she has yet had."

As we were thus gazing and feeling, a shot was fired

from a boat containing some men and women, which, unperceived by us, had glided out from behind the opposite pier; and immediately one of the birds fell into the sea, where it lay fluttering in agony with a broken wing, while its companions fled away with harsh, discordant cries; and in one instant the whole bright scene was changed for us from one of innocence and joy into one of the darkest gloom and misery. It was a murder done in Eden, followed by the instant eclipse of all that made it Paradise. Mary was frantic. Her so lately injured organism gave way under the shock of such a revulsion of feeling. Her impulse was to throw herself into the sea to succour the wounded bird, and it was with difficulty that I restrained her; and only after giving vent to an agony of tears, and pouring on the shooting party a storm of reproaches, at the imminent risk of being given into custody as they landed bearing the bird, now dead, as a trophy, did I succeed in getting her back to the hotel. For the next twenty-four hours her state was one of raving mania.

No incident could be more characteristic of her temperament or of her outlook upon life. The charm and beauty and joy of life were all on the surface and only served to conceal the horror and anguish which lurked beneath. She felt, with the apostle, that all creation groaneth and travaileth together, and to her hyper-sensitive spirit life itself was all too frequently a very hell. One can well understand the ardour with which a spirit like hers pursued the campaign against vivisection. But it is rare indeed to find this temperament joined with a courage which faced the presence of the horrors she so dreaded to go through the entire medical course and qualify as a doctor at a time when obstacles innumerable were placed in the way of women candidates for the profession. It is in connection with this phase of her career that a story is narrated which has attained for her a somewhat unenviable notoriety. This is the record of the boast she is stated herself to have made that she had brought about by her magical powers the death of one of the most prominent supporters of vivisection in its worst form in the medical world. The doctor in question was the well-known Professor Claude Bernard, and the claim that she made will probably be regarded by the occultist as not wanting foundation in fact. The narrative had better be given in her biographer's own words :

It was in mid-February, when, having occasion to visit the *Ecole de Médecine*, I accompanied her thither. It was afternoon. On reaching the place we found it shut up, and a notice on the gate apprised us that the school was closed for the day on account of the obsequies of Professor Claude Bernard. We had not heard even of his illness. A cry, or rather a gasp, of astonishment escaped her, and she exclaimed, "Claude Bernard dead! Claude Bernard dead! Take hold of me! Help me to a seat or I shall fall. Claude Bernard dead! Claude Bernard dead!" The only seat available near was on the stony steps by which we were standing, and I accordingly placed her on these, seeing that emotion had deprived her of all her powers. Once seated she buried her face in her hands, and I stood before her awaiting the result in silence. I knew that such an event could not fail greatly to move her, but no special reason occurred to me. Presently she looked up, her face strangely altered by the intensity of her emotion, and asked me if I remembered what she had told me some weeks ago about Claude Bernard, and her having been provoked to launch her maledictions at him. I remembered perfectly. It was in the latter part of the previous December. Her professor had forced her into a controversy about vivisection, the immediate occasion being some experiments by Claude Bernard on animal heat, made by means of a stove invented by himself, so constructed as to allow of observations being made on animals while being slowly baked to death. Her professor had agreed with her as to the unscientific character and utter uselessness for any medical purpose of such a method of research. But he was altogether insensible to its moral aspects, and in answer to her strong expressions of reprobation, had taken occasion to deliver himself of a tirade against the sentiments generally of morality and religion, and the folly of allowing anything so chimerical to stand in the way, not merely of science, but of any object whatever to which one might be inclined, and setting up a transcendental standard of right and wrong, or recognising any limits to self-gratification saving the physical risks to oneself. Even the feeling which makes a mother weep over her child's suffering he sneered at as hysterical, and gloried in the prospects of the time when science and intellect should be utterly unrestrained by what people call heart and moral conscience, and the only recognised rule should be that of the bodily self.

Thus speaking, he had worked his pupil into a frenzy of righteous indignation, and the vision rose before her of a future when, through the teaching of a materialistic science, society at large had become wholly demonised, even as already were this man and his kind. And seeing in Claude Bernard the foremost living representative and instrument of the fell conspiracy, at once against the human and the divine, to destroy whom would be to rid the earth of one of its worst monsters, she no sooner found herself alone than she rose to her feet, and with passionate energy invoked the wrath of God upon him, at the same moment hurling her whole spiritual being at him with all her might, as if with intent, then and there, to smite him with destruction. And so completely, it seemed to her, had she gone out of herself in the effort that her physical system instantly collapsed, and she fell back powerless on her sofa, where she lay awhile utterly exhausted and unable to move. It was thus that, on rejoining her, I found her, with just sufficient power to recount the experience, and to ask me my opinion as to the possibility of injuring a person at a distance by making, as it were, a spiritual thunderbolt of oneself ; for, if such a thing were possible, and had ever happened, it must, she was convinced, have happened then.

At the moment the discussion on this subject was dropped, but further evidence was subsequently sought which it was hoped would confirm or disprove the idea that Anna Kingsford had been responsible for the great French doctor's death. Eventually, our heroine came across an acquaintance of the deceased Professor in the person of a practical student of occult science. It appeared from his narrative that Claude Bernard was one of the few members of the profession who also took an interest in this subject, which had served as a link between them. He informed Mrs Kingsford that the doctor had described his earliest symptoms to himself, and had regarded them as somewhat mysterious. He was engaged, it appears, in his laboratory in the *Collège de France*, being at the time in his usual health, when he felt himself suddenly struck as if by some poisonous effluvium which he believed to emanate from the subject of his experiment. The effect, instead of passing off, became intensified, and manifested itself in severe internal inflammation, from which he eventually died. The doctors pronounced the complaint to be Bright's disease. This was the disease which Claude Bernard had chiefly endeavoured to investigate by inducing it in animals. The possibility of such an incident is of course familiar to students of occultism, and Paracelsus, with others before and since, have maintained its feasibility. The great German occultist writes that it is possible that the spirit without the help of the body may, " through a fiery will alone, and without a sword, stab and wound others." This is purely in accordance with the general trend of his doctrine, a large part of which is based on the belief that the will is a most potent operator in medicine.

Anna Kingsford was, it is well known, one of the earliest and foremost champions of the movement for women's rights, but the line she took in this movement was supremely sane and wise, and was devoid of all the extravagances which have since brought certain sides of one of the greatest and most important movements of the day into well-deserved contempt. Edward Maitland was in entire sympathy with her in this matter, and in endorsing one of her communications to him observes : " I send you to-day's *Times*, with a report of the debate on the Women's Suffrage Bill, which will show you how much you are needed in that movement. For the debate shows why it does not advance. They are all on the wrong tack, supporters and opponents alike. The franchise is claimed in hostility, not sought in love. The women are demanding it as a means of defence and offence against man, instead of as a means of aiding and perfecting man's work. They want a level platform with man expressly in order to fight him on equal terms. And of course the instinct of the majority of men and women resents such a view." " Justice, in fact, as between men and women, human and animal," was among Anna Kingsford's foremost aims ; for, as her biographer well says : " All injustice was cruelty, and cruelty was for her the one unpardonable sin." " Her love," he adds in a curiously revealing passage, " was all for principles, not for persons. The last thing contemplated by Anna Kingsford was an aggravation of the existing divisions and antagonisms between the sexes." "And," continues Mr Maitland, "so far from accepting the doctrine of the superiority of spinsterhood over wifehood, she regarded it as an assertion of the superiority of non-experience over experience as a means of education." But that which most of all she reprobated was the disposition which led women to despise womanhood itself as an inferior condition, and accordingly to cultivate the masculine at the expense of the feminine side of their nature." "It was by magnifying their womanhood and not by exchanging it for a factitious masculinity that she would have her sex obtain its proper recognition." This recognition no one more ardently desired than herself. She compares the modern woman to Andromeda bound to the rock on the seashore, shackled by the chains of ignorance and a helpless prey to that terrible monster whose name is ennui. "When," she asks, "will Perseus come to deliver the fair Andromeda, to loosen her fetters and to set her free?" Much has happened to better the position of women since this was written, but much yet remains to be done.

All who knew Anna Kingsford unite in testifying to the impression conveyed to them by her striking personality with its originality, freshness, and force, no less than by her many-sidedness and the strange contradictions of her character. Her biographer gives the following description of her appearance at the date when he first met her:

Tall, slender, and graceful in form. Fair and exquisite in complexion. Bright and sunny in expression. The hair long and golden, but the brows and lashes dark and the eyes deep set and hazel, and by turns dreamy and penetrating. The mouth rich, full, and exquisitely formed. The broad brow prominent and sharply cut. The nose delicate, slightly curved, and just sufficiently prominent to give character to the face. And the dress somewhat fantastic as became her looks. Anna Kingsford seemed at first more fairy than human and more child than woman. For though really twenty-seven she appeared scarcely seventeen, and made expressly to be caressed, petted and indulged, and by no means to be taken seriously.

These impressions as regards her character were appreciably modified on subsequent acquaintance, and Mr Maitland observes that " when she warmed to her favourite themes, her whole being radiant with a spiritual light, her utterances were those in turn of a savant, a sage, and a child, each part suiting her as well as if it were her one and only character."

The relationship between the authors of *The Perfect Way* and the founders of the Theosophical Society in the days of its infancy affords matter of no little interest. The basic idea of the Theosophical Society, viz. the harmonising of the esoteric side of all religions, naturally suggested to the promoters of the movement that in the authors of so remarkable a work, they would find a tower of strength, and Madame Blavatsky, in particular, was most anxious to obtain their support and co-operation for the British section of the Society. Eventually, after considerable hesitation, Anna Kingsford responded to the advances made to her, and accepted the presidency of the British section. But the arrangement was not one which was destined to last long. That it was not likely to be a success might, I think, have been readily enough foreseen. Anna Kingsford and Edward Maitland were too uncompromising in their point of view— too positive that the source of their own information could not be impugned, to accept readily the *bona fides* of other and, as they considered, lower oracles. This, however, was by no means all. The attitude of Theosophy in its early days towards Christianity was in the main hostile. To make the esoteric interpretation of this creed the pivot of their teaching was the last idea they contemplated. Madame Blavatsky had attacked Christianity in *Isis Unveiled*. Mr Sinnett was equally unsympathetic. The basis of their actual teaching was an interpretation of Eastern religions, whereas the basis of *The Perfect Way* was an interpretation of Western. Anna Kingsford was just as unhesitating in giving her preference to Christianity as the leaders of Theosophy were in according theirs to Buddhism,

Hinduism, and kindred Oriental philosophies. Mrs Besant's attitude when she joined the Society showed similar preferences. Her early experiences of orthodox Christianity were not such as to bias her in its favour, and it was not until later days that she assumed the mantle of the prophet of *The Perfect Way*, and openly recognised the importance of the esoteric side of Christianity to complete the circle of theosophical teachings. The views with which Theosophy commenced have in the course of time been materially modified, and a curious sidelight is thrown, by a letter of Anna Kingsford's, on the question whether the leaders of this Society had originally adopted the reincarnation hypothesis, or whether this was in the nature of a subsequent development. Mrs Kingsford writes under date 3rd July 1882, to her friend Lady Caithness, alluding to the reception of *The Perfect Way* by the Press :

> After all this reviewing and fault-finding on the part of critics having but a third of the knowledge which has been given to us, there is not a line in *The Perfect Way* which I would alter were the book to be reprinted. The very reviewer—Mr Sinnett—who writes with so much pseudo-authority in the *Theosophist*, has, within a year's time, completely altered his views on at least one important subject—I mean Reincarnation. When he came to see us a year ago in London, he vehemently denied that doctrine, and asserted, with immense conviction, that I had been

altogether deceived in my teaching concerning it. He read a message from *Isis Unveiled* to confute me, and argued long on the subject. He had not then received any instruction from his Hindu guru about it. Now, he has been so instructed, and wrote Mr Maitland a long letter acknowledging the truth of the doctrine which, since seeing us, he has been taught. But he does not yet know all the truth concerning it, and so finds fault with our presentation of that side of it which, as yet, he has not been taught.

Presumably in this matter Mr Sinnett reflected Madame Blavatsky's views, and the fact that he cites *Isis Unveiled* seems to me to leave little doubt in the matter. Surely if he had misunderstood her, H. P. B. would have taken pains to put him right! I think that the date given will fix approximately the period at which official Theosophy was openly converted to the doctrine of Reincarnation. Until that time, if it was not uniformly denied, at least there were wide diversities of opinion, and apparently its opponents mustered more strongly than its supporters. Eventually Anna Kingsford and Edward Maitland founded between them the *Hermetic Society*. This was not destined to a long lease of life, mainly owing to the breakdown of Anna Kingsford's health. But while Theosophy showed the greater vitality, in spite of scandals and discords which might well have shattered it to its base, the teachings of the authors of *The Perfect Way* exercised a profound influence in leavening the mass of Theosophical teaching. Though possessing no little dogmatism in her own intellectual organisation, Anna Kingsford had no great liking for any form of society that taught dogmatically, her idea being that every one must necessarily find out the truth for himself and realise it spiritually from his own individual standpoint. Theosophy was altogether too dogmatic for her, without being dogmatic on her own lines. She was readier to admit the existence of the Mahatmas than to grant the inspired source of their communications. In any case she looked upon their teaching as of a radically lower order than her own, and reflecting those vices and defects which she and Maitland were wont to associate with the denizens of the astral plane. On the subject of communications with such entities, or with those whom she suspected of belonging by nature to this region, she was never tired of inveighing.

The secret (she says) of the opposition made in certain circles to the doctrine set forth in *The Perfect Way* is not far to seek. It is to be found in the fact that the book is, throughout, strenuously opposed to idolatry in all its forms, including that of the popular " spiritualism " of the day, which is, in effect, a revival, under a new guise and with new sanctions, of the ancient cultus known as Ancestor-worship. *The Perfect Way*, on the contrary, insists that truth is accessible only through the illumination, by the Divine Spirit, of man's own soul ; and that precisely in proportion as the individual declines such interior illumination, and seeks to extraneous influences, does he impoverish his own soul and diminish his possibilities of knowledge. It teaches that " Spirits " or " Angels," as their devotees are fond of styling them, are untrustworthy guides, possessed of no positive divine element, and reflecting, therefore, rather than instructing, their interrogators; and that the condition of mind, namely, passivity, insisted on by these " angels " is one to be strenuously avoided, the true attitude for obtaining divine illumination being that of ardent active aspiration, impelled by a resolute determination to know nothing but the Highest. Precisely such a state of passivity, voluntarily induced, and such veneration of and reliance upon " guides " or " controls," are referred to by the Apostle when he says : " But let no man beguile you by a voluntary humility and worshipping of angels." And precisely such exaltation of the personal Jesus, as *The Perfect Way* repudiates and its opponents demand, is by the same Apostle condemned in the words : " Henceforth know we no man after the flesh : yea, though we have known Christ after the flesh, yet now henceforth know we him no more."

Accordingly, as Maitland and Kingsford fell foul of the Theosophical Society on the one hand, they fell foul of the Spiritualists on the other. But the cleavage between Spiritualism and the teaching of *The Perfect Way* was far deeper than that between this teaching and Theosophy. With Theosophy indeed, in its broadest sense, there was nothing in Kingsford and Maitland's teaching that was radically antagonistic. *The Perfect Way* might in fact be accepted to-day, with some reservations on minor points, as a theosophical text-book, and, looked at from this point of view, it is the fullest, the most complete, and the most coherent exposition of Christianity as seen through theosophical spectacles. Anna Kingsford had indeed herself been received into the fold of the Roman Catholic Church, though certainly Roman Catholicism never had a more rebellious or more independent subject. On the doctrine of authority she would never have made concessions, and, without this admission, one fails to see what status the Roman Church can be held to occupy. It is indeed a case of Hamlet without the Prince of Denmark. Her leanings, however, towards the ancient mother of Christian churches was, even in its modified form, gall and wormwood to her partner and collaborator, and in the end it brought about some very unhappy and regrettable scenes in connection with her last hours, and a dispute as to the faith in which she died, which must have been exceedingly painful to all concerned.

Perhaps in no single point does Roman Catholicism present a worse and more undesirable aspect than in the manner in which its missionaries besiege the last hours of the passing soul in the effort to induce its victims, when too weak for resistance, to say " ditto " to the formulæ which their priests pretend to regard as constituting a password to the celestial realms. Certainly, in Anna Kingsford's case, the admission of a Roman Catholic Sister of Mercy to tend her in her last illness was productive of the worst results, troubling her last hours with an unseemly wrangle that did not cease even after her body was consigned to its final resting-place.

A sidelight is thrown on Mrs Kingsford's attitude towards Roman Catholicism by the record of a conversation which her biographer cites her as having had on one occasion with a Roman Catholic priest. She was calling on a Catholic friend on the occasion, and speaking as usual in her very free and self-confident manner with regard to the religious views which she held. Some remark which she made elicited from the priest the rebuke, "Why, my daughter, you have been *thinking*. You should never do that. The Church saves us the trouble and danger of thinking, by telling us what to *believe*. We are only called on to believe. I never think : I dare not. I should go mad if I were to let myself think." Anna Kingsford replied that what she wanted was to understand, and that it was impossible to do this without thinking. Believing without understanding was for her not faith but credulity. "How, except by thinking," she asked, "does one learn whether the Church has the truth ? "

When the Hermetic Society was founded, W. T. Stead was editor of the *Pall Mall Gazette*, and Mrs Kingsford wrote for him an account of the new Society. Stead, with his usual taste for dramatic headlines, entitled it "The Newest Thing in Religions." This was the very last description that its founders were likely to tolerate. Anna Kingsford wrote back an indignant letter of repudiation. "So far," she says, "from being the newest thing in religions, or even claiming to be a religion at all, that at which the Society aims is the recovery of what is really the oldest thing in religion, so old as to have become forgotten and lost—namely, its esoteric and spiritual, and therefore its true signification." Elsewhere she writes of *The Perfect Way* as not purporting to be a new gospel. "Its mission," she says, "is that simply of rehabilitation and re-interpretation undertaken with the view, not of superseding Christianity, but of saving it." She continues :

For, as the deepest and most earnest thinkers of our day are painfully aware, the Gospel of Christendom, as it stands in the Four Evangels, does NOT suffice, uninterpreted, to satisfy the needs of the age, and to furnish a perfect system of thought and rule of life. Christianity —historically preached and understood—has for eighteen centuries filled the world with wars, persecutions, and miseries of all kinds ; and in these days it is rapidly filling it with agnosticism, atheism, and revolt against

KINGSFORD AND MAITLAND

the very idea of God. *The Perfect Way* seeks to consolidate truth in one complete whole, and, by systematising religion, to demonstrate its Catholicity. It seeks to make peace between Science and Faith ; to marry the Intellect with the Intuition ; to bring together East and West, and to unite Buddhist philosophy with Christian love, by demonstrating that the basis of religion is not historical, but spiritual—not physical, but psychic—not local and temporal, but universal and eternal. It avers that the true " Lord Jesus Christ " is no mere historical character, no mere demi-god, by whose material blood the souls of men are washed white, but " the hidden man of the heart," continually born, crucified, ascending and glorified in the interior Kingdom of the Christian's own Spirit. A scientific age rightly refuses to be any longer put off with data which are more than dubious, and logic which morality and philosophy alike reject. A deeper, truer, more real religion is needed for an epoch of thought, and for a world familiar with Biblical criticism and revision— a religion whose foundations no destructive agnosticism can undermine, and in whose structure no examination, however searching, shall be able to find flaw or blemish. It is only by rescuing the Gospel of Christ from the externals of history, persons, and events, and by vindicating its essential significance, that Christianity can be saved from the destruction which inevitably overtakes all idolatrous creeds. There is not a word in *The Perfect Way* at variance with the spirit of the Gospel of the " Lord Jesus Christ."

Nothing shows the method adopted in their Gospel of Interpretation by the two authors more clearly than their teaching with regard to the story of the Garden of Eden and the Fall of Man. It is curious how literally this story has been taken through many ages of the Church's history, in view of the fact that such a writer as Origen in the early days of the infant Church observed that : " No one in his time would be so foolish as to take this allegory as a description of actual fact." Kingsford and Maitland refer the interpretation firstly to the Church, and secondly to individual man. " The conscience," they say, " set over the human reason as its guide, overseer, and ruler, whether, in the general, as the Church, or in the particular, as the individual, falls, when, listening to the suggestions of the lower nature, she desires, seeks, and at length defiles herself with, the ambitions and falsehoods of this present world." " Ceasing to be a trustworthy guide she becomes herself serpent and seducer to the human reason, leading him into false paths until, if she have her way, she will end by plunging him into the lowest depths of abject ignorance, there to be devoured by the brood of unreason and to be annihilated for ever. For she is now no longer the true wife, Faith, she has become the wanton, Superstition." On the other hand, " the Church at her best, unfallen, is the glass to the lamp of Truth, guarding the sacred flame within and transmitting unimpaired to her children the light received upon its inner surface." Hitherto this fall has been the common fate of all Churches. " Thus fallen and degraded, the Church becomes a church of this world, greedy of worldly dignities, emoluments, and dominion, intent on foisting on the belief of her votaries in the name of authority fables and worse than fables—a Church jealous of the letter which killeth, ignorant of, or bitterly at enmity with, the spirit which giveth life."

We now come to the interpretation of the Fall as applied to individual Man. This is allegorically described as " the lapse of heavenly beings from their first happy estate and their final redemption by means of penance done through incarnation in the flesh." The authors tell us that this imagined lapse is a parable designed to veil and preserve a truth. This truth is the Creative Secret, the projection of Spirit into matter, the descent of substance into Maya, or illusion. From a cosmic standpoint " the Tree of Divination or Knowledge becomes Motion or the Kalpa—the period of Existence as distinguished from Being; the Tree of Life is Rest or the Sabbath, the Nirvâna. Adam is Manifestation; the Serpent—no longer of the lower, but of the higher sphere—is the celestial Serpent or Seraph of Heavenly Counsel." By the Tree of Divination of Good and Evil in this interpretation must be understood that condition by means of which Spirit projected into appearance becomes manifested under the veil of Maya, a necessary condition for the evolution of the individual, but carrying with it its own inevitable perils. It is not, say our authors, because matter is in itself evil that the soul's descent into it constitutes a fall. It is because to the soul matter is a forbidden thing. By quitting her own proper condition and descending into matter she takes upon herself matter's limitations. It is no particular act that constitutes sin. Sin does not consist in fulfilling any of the functions of nature. Sin consists in acting without or against the Spirit, and in not seeking the divine sanction for everything that is done. Sin, in fact, is of the soul, and it is due to the soul's inclination to the things of sense. To regard an act as *per se* sinful is materialism and idolatry. For in doing so we invest that which is physical with a spiritual attribute, and this is of the essence of idolatry.

Adam signifies the manifested personality, or man, and is only complete when Eve, his soul, is added to him as helpmeet. When Eve takes of the fruit and enjoys it, she turns away from her higher spiritual self to seek for pleasure in the things of her lower self, and in doing so she draws Adam down with her till they both become sensual and debased. The sin which commences in the thought of the soul, Eve, thus becomes subsequently developed into action through the energy of the body or masculine part, Adam. One of the inevitable

results of the soul's enslavement to matter is its liability to extinction. In eating of the fruit Adam and Eve absorb the seeds of mortality. As Milton says :
> They engorged without restraint,
> And knew not, eating Death.

The soul in her own nature is immortal, but the lower she sinks into matter the weaker becomes her vitality. A continuous downward course must therefore end in the extinction of the individual—not of course of the Divine Ray, which returns to the Source whence it came. It is well to bear in mind that man is a dual being, not masculine or feminine only, but both. This, of course, applies equally to man whether manifested in a male or female body. One side is more predominant in man and the other in woman, but this does not imply absence of the other side, but merely its subordination. The man who has nothing, or next to nothing, of the woman in him, is no true man, and the woman who has nothing of the man in her, is no true woman. Man, whether man or woman, consists of male and female, Reason and Intuition, and is therefore essentially twofold. Owing to the duality of his constitution, every doctrine relating to man has a dual significance and application. Thus the sacred books not only present an historical narrative of events occurring in time, but have a spiritual significance of a permanent character in regard to which the element of time has no meaning. In this sense Scripture is a record of that which is always taking place.

Thus, the Spirit of God, which is original Life, is always moving upon the face of the waters, or heavenly deep, which is original Substance. And the One, which consists of these two, is always putting forth alike the Macrocosm of the universe and the Microcosm of the individual, and is always making man in the image of God, and placing him in a garden of innocence and perfection, the garden of his own unsophisticated nature. And man is always falling away from that image and quitting that garden for the wilderness of sin, being tempted by the serpent of sense, his own lower element. And from this condition and its consequences he is always being born of a pure virgin—dying, rising and ascending into heaven.

This, in brief, is one of the most essential portions of the new Gospel of Interpretation. It exemplifies the method adopted throughout which is that to which we are accustomed to apply the word "Hermetic." It is both Christian and pre-Christian, for it is the interpretation of the meaning of life, which was the Key to the ancient Gnostic faiths which, subsisting before Christianity, became incorporated in the Christian teaching. New generations and races of men require the old truths to be put before them in a new guise. This was so when Christianity first came to birth, but in the days of Jesus Christ there were many things which the

Prophet of Nazareth had to say to his disciples, but which, as he told them, they were then too weak to understand. The mystical interpretation of Christian truth fell on deaf ears then. Re-stated and re-interpreted, after a lapse of 1900 years, is it too much to hope that it may no longer prove "to the Gentiles foolishness, and to the Jews a rock of offence"?

DATE DUE

MAY 22 '79			
MAY 28			
MAY 28 '93			
APR 19 '95			

GAYLORD · PRINTED IN U.S.A.

1000084811
HOUGHTON COLLEGE LIBRARY - Houghton, NY